GRACE AND TRUTH

By the same author

Jesus Christ in the Old Testament (1965)
Studies in the Pastoral Epistles (1968)
Studies in Paul's Technique and Theology (1974)

GRACE AND TRUTH

A Study in the Doctrine of the Incarnation

ANTHONY TYRRELL HANSON

LONDON

SPCK

1975

First published 1975
by SPCK
Holy Trinity Church
Marylebone Road
London NW1 4DU

Printed in Great Britain by
The Camelot Press Ltd, Southampton

SBN 281 02840 0 cased
SBN 281 02848 6 paper

To
Kathryn Prestt
and
Wendy Sproston
to whom the argument
of this book
was first set forth

CONTENTS

ACKNOWLEDGEMENTS

I wish to acknowledge the help which I received from Mr R. J. Brookes and his colleagues in the S.P.C.K. publishing department and also to express my gratitude to Mr Frank Lyons, M.A., Head of the Department of Theology in Endsleigh College, Hull, for his much appreciated assistance in reading the proofs, and also to my wife and my son Philip for invaluable help in compiling the indexes.

A. T. H.

Biblical quotations from the Revised Standard Version of the Bible, copyrighted 1946, 1952, and 1957 by the Division of Christian Education of the National Council of the Churches of Christ in the United States of America, are used by permission.

Thanks are due to the following for permission to quote from copyright sources:

T. & T. Clark Ltd: *Church Dogmatics*, vol. 1, by Karl Barth, translated by G. W. Bromiley and T. F. Torrance.

Faber & Faber Ltd: *God Was in Christ*, by D. M. Baillie.

Darton, Longman & Todd Ltd: *Theological Investigations*, vols. 1, 3, and 4, by Karl Rahner.

James Nisbet & Co. Ltd and Harper & Row Publishers Inc.: *The Word Incarnate*, by W. N. Pittenger.

SCM Press Ltd and The Westminster Press: *Jesus—God and Man*, by Wolfhart Pannenberg, translated by L. L. Wilkins and D. A. Priebe. Copyright © MCMLXVIII The Westminster Press. Used by permission.

ABBREVIATIONS

e.	edition
ET	English Translation
LXX	the Septuagint
NEB	New English Bible
NTS	*New Testament Studies*
RSV	Revised Standard Version
RV	Revised Version
TEV	Today's English Version
TWNT	*Theologisches Wörterbuch zum Neuen Testament*

TRANSLITERATION OF GREEK
AND VERSIONS OF THE BIBLE

In transliterating Greek words I have followed the scheme advocated by H. Leclerque in his article 'A Note on the Transliteration of New Testament Greek' in *NTS* (January 1973), pp. 187–9. Latin quotations are also put in italics.

All quotations from the Bible, unless otherwise indicated, are from the Revised Standard Version of 1946, 1952, and 1957.

INTRODUCTION

This book is the result of my own intellectual quest. It is very
much an example of Anselm's *fides quaerens intellectum*. My
studies in the New Testament have been mainly concerned with
Paul, with the post-Pauline literature including Hebrews, and
with the Fourth Gospel. From these I have become convinced that
some sort of a doctrine of incarnation is necessary for those who
wish to be faithful to the witness of the New Testament. In any
case traditional Christianity has always been based on a doctrine
of the incarnation of the Word of God. Thus, both my own
studies and my respect for Christian tradition pointed towards the
necessity for such a doctrine. But the more I thought about the
problem, the more difficult I found it to reconcile the traditional
Christian doctrine with what the New Testament evidence seemed
to suggest and with what could be credibly expressed in terms
intelligible to us today.

During my theological formation I was well instructed in the
traditional account of the incarnation of God in Jesus Christ. I
distinctly remember being told that the Word of God, when he
assumed human nature, assumed impersonal humanity: that
Jesus Christ did not possess a human personality; that God
became man in Jesus Christ, but that he did not become *a* man.
In other words, I was taught to believe in the hypostatic union,
that the Word of God appeared himself in human nature which
he joined ontologically, substantially to himself. Naturally, with
this went the Chalcedonian doctrine that there are in Jesus Christ
two natures, a divine and a human, inseparably united but not
confused.

Two considerations have persuaded me that this traditional
Christology is incredible—for me at any rate, and probably for
many other thinking people who have been brought up in the

intellectual atmosphere of the Western world. The first is this: the Chalcedonian Christology is heavily dependent on the picture of Christ presented in the Fourth Gospel. But, if we are to be intellectually honest, we can no longer treat the Fourth Gospel as a straightforward historical record of the life and teaching of Jesus of Nazareth. We can no longer bring forward as evidence in favour of the Chalcedonian Christology the claim, for instance, that Jesus said 'I and the Father are one' or 'Before Abraham was, I am'. This drastically alters our understanding of the christo- logical problem. Such a conclusion has been accepted among scholars in Germany for at least a hundred years, but it is surprising how long it has taken to be accepted in English theology. For instance, in *Essays Catholic and Critical*, which was written less than half a century ago, though E. C. Hoskyns is certainly aware that the Fourth Gospel cannot safely be used as primary evidence for what Jesus taught, J. K. Mozley in the same volume seems to be quite unaware of this.[1] And as we shall be seeing, Relton, writing in 1934, uses the Fourth Gospel as evidence without any demur. It is one of the great virtues of the late W. R. Matthews' little book on the doctrine of the incarnation that he squarely faces the problem presented by the Fourth Gospel;[2] but he published it at a time when the theological tide was still running strongly against him and his book seems to have been largely ignored. It is hardly necessary to add that doubts about the historical accuracy of the Fourth Gospel have so far made almost no impression at all upon the English pulpit: neither clergy nor laity have any hesita- tion in expounding the material in the Fourth Gospel as if it was straightforward reportage; an adverse judgement on the historical value of John's Gospel does most certainly not entail a dismissal of its importance for a doctrine of the incarnation. No one who troubles to read this book to the end can possibly have any doubt but that I consider the Fourth Gospel to be an essential witness when we come to formulate our account of the significance of Jesus Christ.

The second consideration that has made the traditional account of the doctrine of the incarnation incredible for me has been the growing conviction that in our account of Jesus Christ we must begin from the assumption that, whatever else he was, he was a real human personality. He was, in fact, a man. But I cannot reconcile this with the Chalcedonian Christology. I know that the attempt has been made, notably by Schoonenberg, but it certainly does not convince me. As I understand it, the orthodox Fathers of the Church did not regard Jesus Christ as exhibiting a human personality. Admittedly their concept of personality was deficient and their language sometimes ambiguous, but I do not believe that they were even trying with imperfect tools to express what we mean by a human personality. Had we been able to explain to them what we mean by it, I do not think they would have accepted that such a phenomenon is to be found in Jesus Christ. I do not think that the concept of hypostatic union, the Word uniting himself metaphysically to human nature, is compatible with the belief that Jesus Christ exhibited a real human personality. Throughout this work I have used the phrase 'God-man Christology' to designate the Chalcedonian approach to the doctrine of the incarnation. I hope I will be forgiven for this, since it is a convenient abbreviation. I know that some theologians who reject the Chalcedonian Christology, notably D. M. Baillie, use the phrase 'God-man' for Jesus Christ; but I do not think it is really appropriate to D. M. Baillie's theology of the incarnation. I propose therefore to use it to indicate the traditional Christology of hypostatic union.

I have attempted, then, to formulate a doctrine of the incarnation of the Word of God in Jesus Christ that is firmly based on the Scriptures but does not invoke a theory of hypostatic union or of an impersonal humanity. Of course, I am not the first person in modern times to attempt this; but I believe that, though I owe a great deal to some modern theologians, notably D. M. Baillie and W. N. Pittenger, I have advanced beyond their positions in certain respects, especially in the concept of Jesus Christ as the revelation of the divine grace and truth, and also in the presentation of the divinity as revealed in the humanity. I would be so bold as to claim that my account of the incarnation is at least as firmly rooted in Scripture as is that of the Chalcedonian Fathers, and indeed that it is an improvement on their account to the extent that it can show a much stronger foundation in the Old Testament.

In the first chapter I present the idea of Jesus Christ as the revelation of God's grace and truth as it meets us in the Fourth Gospel, in Paul, in the Gospel of Matthew, and in the teaching of Jesus himself. This is linked up with the revelation of God under the old dispensation. In Chapter 2 we consider the revelation of the divinity in the humanity as we find it in Paul, in Hebrews, and in John. In Chapter 3 we explore the suggestion that the revelation of God through human obedience and suffering is a theme that can be traced in Israel's history before the coming of Christ. In Chapter 4 we consider a number of problems which this account of the incarnation must face, of which the two major ones are the doctrine of the pre-existence of Christ as found in the New Testament, and the necessity of being able to recognize God in Christ. We also consider the doctrine of the Trinity in the light of the incarnation doctrine we have expounded. In the last chapter we discuss the traditional Chalcedonian doctrine and some of its modern defenders; and we also assess the views of some modern theologians, both British and Continental, who have written on this subject.

1

JESUS CHRIST AS GRACE
AND TRUTH

We begin with that passage in the New Testament which is more explicitly concerned with the doctrine of the incarnation than any other, John 1.14–18. We quote part of it as follows:

> And the Word became flesh and dwelt among us, full of grace and truth; we have beheld his glory, glory as of the only Son from the Father. . . . And from his fulness have we all received, grace upon grace. For the law was given through Moses; grace and truth came through Jesus Christ. No one has ever seen God; the only Son, who is in the bosom of the Father, he has made him known.

We have here a remarkable emphasis on 'grace and truth' as revealed in Jesus Christ, a reference to the law given on Sinai by the mediation of Moses, and a mysterious insistence that no man has ever seen God. There is in the Old Testament one passage where all these elements come together, and, as I believe, we can only fully understand what John is saying when we read what he has to say in the light of that passage. It is to Exod. 34 that we must turn if we are to pursue John's reference. Exod. 34 is part of a long narrative at the beginning of which Moses makes the very bold request that he should be permitted to see God's glory (Exod. 33.18). God replies that no man can see God's face and live, but he does promise that 'you shall see my back' (33.23). Accordingly Moses is placed in a cleft in the rock on Sinai. Then the narrative proceeds (34.6–7):

> The Lord passed before him and proclaimed, 'The Lord, the Lord, a God merciful and gracious, slow to anger, and

abounding in steadfast love and faithfulness, keeping steadfast
love for thousands, forgiving iniquity and transgression and
sin, but who will by no means clear the guilty . . .'

There follows what many scholars believe to be the earliest version
of the covenant law.

Here then is a revelation of God's nature, which is what 'glory'
means in this context; and at the heart of that revelation is a
phrase which John actually quotes. The phrase is translated by the
RSV as:

abounding in steadfast love and faithfulness.

The Hebrew consists of only three words:

rab ḥesed we'emeth.

This is precisely rendered in John 1.14 with

plērēs kharitos kai alētheias.[1]

Our familiar translation 'full of grace and truth' tends rather to
divert attention from the fact that this is a quotation from Exod.
34.6, since *ḥesed* is not normally rendered with 'grace'. But John's
word *kharis* in fact is occasionally used in the LXX as a translation
of *ḥesed*. John must have had *plērēs kharitos kai alētheias* in his
Greek version of Exod. 34.6, or else, as I believe is perfectly
possible, deliberately translated the phrase from the Hebrew
himself. At any rate his intention is clear: the same God who
showed himself to Moses at the giving of the law has now
manifested himself in Jesus Christ and can be recognized as
manifesting the same essential characteristics, grace and truth, or
better still love and faithfulness. But the reference to the impossibility of seeing God suggests that John is saying even more than
this: no man has ever seen God. But on the occasion recorded in
Exod. 33—34 Moses saw God; therefore he whom Moses saw
from the cleft in the rock was not the invisible Father, but the
pre-existent Son, whose function it is always to make God
known.[2] The contrast therefore in John 1.14–18 is not between the
law revealed through Moses on Sinai and God revealed through
Jesus Christ: it is between grace and truth (God's essential nature)
revealed in a temporary and limited way on Sinai and the same

God revealed fully in Jesus Christ. The reference to Moses in John 1.17 is to underline the limitations of the law dispensation. All that Moses could do was to mediate the law-code to Israel. What God does is to reveal himself through the Word, partially on Sinai, fully in Jesus Christ.

We have claimed that the phrase 'full of grace and truth' indicates the revelation of God's essential nature; some evidence from the Old Testament tradition must be given in order to establish this. The earliest meaning of the word *ḥesed* is defined as 'the mutual liability of those who are relatives, friends, master or servant, or belonging together in any other way'. Glueck defines *ḥesed* as 'conduct corresponding to a mutual relationship of rights and duties'. The other Hebrew noun *'emeth* meant originally 'trustworthiness' and is often used for 'stability, constancy, enduringness'. As Glueck remarks, 'wherever *ḥesed* appears together with *'emeth* or *'emūnah*, the quality of loyalty inherent in the concept *ḥesed* is emphasized'.[3] The two words frequently occur in the Hebrew Scriptures as a description both of God's character and of the corresponding conduct which God requires of man. There is a very remarkable passage in Hos. 4.1 in which these words occur:

> Hear the word of the Lord, O people of Israel;
> for the Lord has a controversy with the inhabitants of the land.
> There is no faithfulness (*'emeth*) or kindness (*ḥesed*),
> and no knowledge of God in the land.

It is no coincidence that the absence of faithfulness and kindness among men is connected with the absence of knowledge of God. Weingreen insists that instead of 'knowledge of God' we should translate 'acknowledgement of God'. He writes 'what the prophet is denouncing is the total abandonment of all religious and moral principles'.[4] A. Weiser well comments: 'God demands a life which is in accordance with his own life.'[5] It is very significant that one of the first of the great prophets should single out *ḥesed* and *'emeth* as sure indications of God's character. We have chosen this passage out of others that could be quoted from the prophets because it intimately connects man's behaviour with God's character, and because, coming as it does at the beginning of the activity of the canonical prophets, it demonstrates strikingly what

B

is considered to be the essential element in God's revelation of himself to Israel.

The phrase is very frequent in the Psalms; in Ps. 89, for instance, it almost constitutes a refrain; and in Ps. 85 the revelation of the divine love and faithfulness is a feature of the coming messianic era. But we will confine ourselves to one more passage in the Old Testament, Jonah 4.2–3. Jonah has realized that because the Ninevites have repented God does not intend to carry out the judgement on the city which Jonah had proclaimed. This annoys Jonah intensely and he says:

> I pray thee, Lord, is not this what I said when I was yet in my country? That is why I made haste to flee to Tarshish; for I knew that thou art a gracious God and merciful, slow to anger, and abounding in steadfast love and repentest of evil. Therefore now, O Lord, take my life from me, for it is better for me to die than to live.

There can be no doubt that Jonah is referring to the great theophany described in Exod. 34.6–7, though in fact he does not mention *'emeth*. But he does use the words *rab ḥesed*, 'abounding in steadfast love', from Exod. 34.6. Bewer suggests that Jonah is angry not out of personal vanity but because the Ninevites have been spared: 'He needed no special divine revelation, for it was in accord with Yahweh's character and prophetic doctrine.'[6] Rudolph draws an interesting parallel with Jeremiah:[7] he too had to deliver a message which he would have preferred to avoid. But we should point out that Jeremiah's pain and protest had exactly the opposite motivation to Jonah's: Jonah protested at having to proclaim a message which would lead to a display of God's mercy; Jeremiah disliked preaching a message which would bring judgement. The author of the Book of Jonah, a brilliant and subtle writer if ever there was one, represents Jonah as picking out what he regards as the fatal weakness in God's character, his tendency to show mercy. One must surely acknowledge the importance of this passage for our study: the Book of Jonah does not stand in the orthodox tradition of late Judaism, but it was taken up by the early Church, probably acting on a hint from Jesus himself. The author of the Book has boldly claimed, not only that mercy is the determinative characteristic of God's nature, but that this mercy is shown towards Gentiles as well as Jews—a true indication, we must surely conclude, of what was to come.

The representation of God as 'abounding in steadfast love and faithfulness' did not fall out of sight during the intertestamental period. The author of the Book of Wisdom can write:

> But thou, our God, art kind and true,
> patient, and ruling all things in mercy.[8]

And the phrase occurs in the Qumran documents. The divine revelation on Sinai narrated in Exod. 33—34 held, as we might expect, very great importance for rabbinic Judaism. It was from Exod. 34.6–7 that the famous thirteen attributes of God were derived; but his mercy (*hesed*) receives special attention. One rabbi asks: 'What [was the purpose] when Scripture wrote "long-suffering" [in the dual form] where the singular might well have been used? But [this is the purport]: long-suffering towards the righteous and long-suffering also towards the wicked.' In another Tractate we read the following comment: 'The Lord, the Lord: I am the Eternal before a man sins and the same after a man sins and repents.' M. Simon points out that according to the famous medieval commentator Rashi the divine Name (here translated of course by 'the Lord') designates the divine attitude of mercy. So the repetition of the name here means both *hesed* and *'emeth*: God is merciful before and merciful after.[9] We might also detect in rabbinic tradition a tendency to qualify the directness with which Moses is represented in the sacred text as seeing God. The Palestinian Targum paraphrases Exod. 33.23 thus: 'And I will cause the hosts of angels who stand and minister before me to pass by, and will make known the oracle; for the glory of my Shekinah thou art not able to behold.'[10] This tendency, which may well have been known to John, would serve in his eyes to enhance by contrast the directness and reality of God's revelation in Christ.

Thus John has taken two leading characteristics of God, revealed at a moment which came to be regarded as almost the classical revelation of God at the time of the giving of the law on Sinai, and isolated them as also revealed in Jesus Christ. It is important to note that, for the purpose of establishing our doctrine of the incarnation, it is not necessary to show that mercy and truth constituted an exhaustive, exclusive, or invariable description of God in the Old Testament. This is certainly not correct: one could point to many passages in the Old Testament where other qualities of God are emphasized, such as wrath, judgement, holiness, jealousy, etc. Nor is it necessary to deny a development in Israel's understanding of God in the course of her history. For our purpose it is quite sufficient if we can establish that mercy and truth were leading characteristics of God, and that the theophany narrated in Exod. 33—34 came to be regarded as something like the normative revelation of God's nature. Nor need we claim that everything said about God in the Old Testament was fulfilled in Christ.[11] In the life, death, and resurrection of Jesus Christ these characteristics were thrown into strong relief, identified as the essential qualities of God's nature, so that Jesus Christ acted as a screen through which only what was true and authentic in God's nature penetrated to the apprehension of Christians. In this way Jesus Christ is both recognizable as the image and supreme revelation of God and also acts himself as the criterion for what was truly known of God during Israel's history. We should also add that, when we are thinking in terms of revelation, we should not strictly speaking treat 'mercy' and 'truth' as two parallel attitudes of God. The word *'emeth*, as Glueck has said, indicates a quality of the *hesed*: it is lasting, faithful love. In other words *hesed* is a genuine revelation of God's nature, for it denotes him as he always is.

At the same time we can claim that this approach to the doctrine of the incarnation gives a more satisfactory Old Testament basis to the doctrine than that which traditional Christology provides. When asked for Old Testament foundations for the doctrine of the incarnation, traditional Christian apologists have usually been content to cite specifically messianic passages, or else to supply proof texts such as Gen. 3.15 or Isa. 7.14. The messianic texts do not normally suggest an incarnation, and the proof texts would carry no conviction at all for anyone who was not prepared to take a literalistic view of Scripture. The doctrine of *hesed* and *'emeth* which we have been outlining does at least show how a doctrine of incarnation in this sense fits naturally on to certain important themes in the Old Testament. Besides this, we do later on make use of other elements in the Old Testament, to be found in Jeremiah and Second Isaiah.

John, as we have seen, brings out quite deliberately the revelation of 'grace and truth' in Jesus Christ. This is why we have chosen the prologue to the Fourth Gospel as the best starting-point. But Paul in his own way, and much less explicitly, makes exactly the same claim. We have to examine two passages in Romans, 9.14–16 and 15.7–9. In the ninth chapter of Romans Paul is wrestling with the difficult but vital question: how is it that the Christian Church has inherited the promises which God originally gave to the Jews? In 9.6f he points out that God's promise has not failed; the fact that the promises have been inherited by only a relatively small section of Israel is no new phenomenon. God has always worked through a chosen remnant. He chooses people according to his own purpose and not according to human merit. This is well illustrated in the case of Esau and Jacob, one of whom was rejected and one chosen while they were still in the womb (verses 10–13). But this raises the question of God's justice. Is God unjust? Not at all, says Paul, but

> he says to Moses, 'I will have mercy on whom I have mercy, and I will have compassion on whom I have compassion.' So it depends not upon man's will or exertion, but upon God's mercy.

Paul goes on to cite the case of Pharaoh, who was raised up by God to be an example of judgement. And Paul concludes with the grim sentence in verse 18:

> So then he has mercy upon whomever he wills, and he hardens the heart of whomever he wills.

At first glance it seems as if Paul is making God out to be an arbitrary tyrant: he arbitrarily chooses Jacob and rejects Esau. He arbitrarily hardens Pharaoh's heart. But if we look at Paul's argument in longer perspective, we can perceive that this is not Paul's meaning. He is arguing in fact that all God's actions, difficult though it may be to interpret them at the time, are inspired by the one motive of mercy. This is the point of verse 16. In verse 14 Paul has asked, Is God unjust? He replies with a verse from the theophany narrative of Exod. 33—34, where God promises that Moses will see his glory:

I will make all my goodness pass before you, and will proclaim
before you my name 'The Lord'; and I will be gracious to
whom I will be gracious, and will show mercy on whom I will
show mercy (Exod. 33.19).

In other words, Moses will realize when he sees God's glory that it
is God's very nature to have mercy. He is the God of mercy. This
is what Paul is seeking to convey in Rom. 9.16. It is possible that
the RSV translation in this verse does not bring this out as clearly
as it might: 'It depends . . . upon God's mercy.' The Greek is
tou eleōntos theou 'the pitying God'. The present participle defines
the noun: God is defined and characterized by mercy. This is the
ultimate motive behind all his actions.[12] The fact that the proof
of God's mercy is drawn from the theophany passage in Exod.
33—34 is surely an indication that Paul sees mercy as constituting
the most authentic characteristic of God's nature.

So far Paul has not explicitly mentioned Jesus Christ in this
context. For that we must turn to the second passage, Rom. 15.7–9.
It runs as follows:

Welcome one another, therefore, as Christ has welcomed you,
for the glory of God. For I tell you that Christ became a servant
to the circumcised to show God's truthfulness, in order to
confirm the promises given to the patriarchs, and in order
that the Gentiles might glorify God for his mercy.

Here 'truthfulness' translates *alētheia* and 'mercy' renders *eleos*,
so both *hesed* and *'emeth* are found here. We should notice that
Paul in this passage is concerned with the whole design of God,
of which the incarnation is the centre. These verses form part of an
entire section in which Paul is exhorting his correspondents to
show mutual love and to welcome each other; he cites the example
of Christ who did not think of his own advantage but 'welcomed'
us by taking on him our humanity, even to the extent of becoming
a servant to the Jewish people. In verses 8 and 9 Paul describes this
in terms of the truth or fidelity and of the mercy of God; Christ
by his coming confirmed the truth of God's promises and the
result was that the Gentiles experienced the mercy of God. Thus
the divine mercy and truth were both expressed in the career of
Jesus Christ. So Paul as well as John, though not as clearly as

John, represents Jesus Christ as expressing and revealing the mercy and the faithfulness of God.[13]

In the First Gospel also Jesus is represented as the eschatological manifestation of God's *ḥesed*, so that Matthew in effect has the same approach as Paul and John. Twice in his Gospel Matthew represents Jesus as quoting from Hosea, in Matt. 9.13 and 12.7. The citation is of Hos. 6.6 and is given in the form:

I desire mercy and not sacrifice.

The word 'mercy' represents *eleos* in the Greek. In Hosea it occurs in this form:

For I desire steadfast love and not sacrifice,
the knowledge of God, rather than burnt offerings.

In Hos. 6.6 the original word is *ḥesed* and 'knowledge of God' translates the same phrase as occurs in Hos. 4.1, so that Matthew's quotation very closely reproduces Hosea's teaching in Hos. 4.1. In Matt. 9.13 the quotation is attached to the 'physician' logion and occurs in the context of a challenge to Jesus because he mixes with publicans and sinners. In 12.7 it comes at the end of the episode in which Jesus vindicates his disciples for plucking corn on the sabbath. Very few modern commentators would suggest that in this citation of Hosea we have the authentic words of Jesus, though not all are agreed that it was actually added by the author of the First Gospel. Bultmann suggests that the quotation was provided by the early church tradition, 'unless it derives from Matthew's distinctive learning in the law'.[14] The comment of the distinguished Jewish scholar C. G. Montefiore is worth quoting: 'The motive of pity here given for Jesus' exceptional conduct is quite in keeping with his character.'[15]

Even more remarkable is the conclusion which scholars draw from these citations from Hosea in Matthew's Gospel. Lohmeyer suggests that the Hosea quotation really underlines all that Jesus came to do for sinners. Jesus' meal with publicans and sinners is a better sacrifice than that which the priests perform, so that in this meal we see God's eschatological will, and the Hosea quotation becomes a sort of prophecy of what God will require in the last days. He writes: 'The word from Hosea is a christological citation.' Jesus has brought the word to fulfilment by eating with sinners, and this saying vindicates the Lord's Supper against Pharisaic objections.[16] Another scholar says that the quotation of Hosea 'denotes a dispensation, an emancipation'. God himself is the merciful one, and the sabbath commandment should be looked at from that point of view.[17]

Entirely in line with this view of Jesus is another passage in the First Gospel, Matt. 23.23:

> Woe to you, scribes and Pharisees, hypocrites! for you tithe mint and dill and cummin, and have neglected the weightier matters of the law, justice and mercy and faith; these you ought to have done, without neglecting the others.

The words 'justice and mercy and faith' translate *krisis* and *eleos* and *pistis*. The Lucan parallel occurs in Luke 11.42, where the crucial sentence runs:

> . . . and neglect justice and the love of God.

The key words in Greek are *krisis* and *agapē* respectively. The fact that there is a Lucan parallel shows that this comes from the material common to Matthew and Luke but not found in Mark, which for want of a better hypothesis we shall continue to call Q. Bultmann is unwontedly sanguine about the authenticity of the material here. He writes: 'But the oldest material is clearly in the brief conflict sayings which express in a parable-like form the attitude of Jesus to Jewish piety,'[18] and among these sayings he includes Matt. 23.23.

Thus Matthew in his own very different way has made the same claim about Jesus that Paul and John make: in Jesus a new dispensation of mercy or love has been inaugurated and in his ministry God has been newly revealed as the God of mercy. This last passage which we considered, Matt. 23.23, must raise the question how far this claim was reflected in the mind of Jesus himself; and to this question we must turn presently.

But first we should observe that the presentation of Jesus as the full revelation of the God who was revealed to Moses on the rock is not confined to the Gospels, Paul, and John. Traces can be found in the rest of the New Testament. Boismard draws our attention to Heb. 2.17, where Christ is described as 'a merciful and faithful high priest'.[19] There is also a remarkable passage in the Pastoral

Epistles which claims our attention (I regard the Pastorals as deutero-Pauline for the most part). It is 1 Tim. 1.13–16:

> but I received mercy because I had acted ignorantly in unbelief, and the grace of our Lord overflowed for me with the faith and love that are in Christ Jesus. . . . but I received mercy for this reason, that in me, as the foremost, Jesus Christ might display his perfect patience for an example to those who were to believe in him for eternal life.

This is an interesting passage, not least because it shares so many words in common with the description of the theophany in Exod. 34.6. It would be possible to draw up a list of these parallels thus:

EXODUS 34.6	I TIMOTHY 1.13–16
a God merciful and gracious	I received mercy . . . the grace of our Lord overflowed with the
abounding in stead-fast love	faith and love that are in Christ Jesus that . . . Jesus Christ
slow to anger	might display his perfect patience.

The last parallel is obscured in the RSV translation: 'patience' in 1 Tim. 1.16 renders *makrothumia* and the Septuagint translation for the Hebrew 'slow to anger' is *makrothumos*. It might seem forced to compare the *'emeth* of Exod. 34.6 with the faith (*pistis*) of 1 Tim. 1.14, since 'faith' in 1 Tim. 1.14 might seem to refer to man's faith in God. But in fact this is by no means clear. Spicq, for instance, describes faith and love in this context as 'the fruits of Christ or his direct emanations', and Jeremias calls them 'the outflowing of the divine mercy'.[20] One might very well conclude that we have here a Christian version of Ps. 85.10: in the messianic era *ḥesed* and *'emeth* are to be equally an expression of the divine nature revealed and of man's response to it.

In the Pastoral Epistles there is no hesitation in describing Christ as God, so undoubtedly the intention in this passage in 1 Timothy is to present Christ as God's revelation and to emphasize that in him the mercy, and probably also the faithfulness, of God is uniquely displayed, as occurred on Sinai. Kelly actually gives a cross-reference to Exod. 34.6.[21] If we date the Pastoral Epistles as having been written some time about the end of the first century, we may appropriately regard this passage as confirming what both Paul and John claim to have occurred in the career of Jesus Christ: he fulfilled and completed what God revealed of himself on Sinai. There God was revealed as being indeed full of grace and truth, but also as one who is 'long-suffering', a word which suggests that there could be an end to his patience. The author of the Pastorals, on the strength of God's revelation in Jesus Christ, boldly claims that there is in fact no limit to his forbearance. His mercy is infinite.

Before we turn to an examination of what Jesus himself taught about the mercy of God, we ought to make one point. We are not claiming, and we do not need to claim, that the presentation of Jesus Christ as the unique revelation of the mercy and faithfulness of God necessarily exhausts all that the writers of the New Testament have to say about his person and significance. Such a claim would be absurd. Both Paul and John have more to say about him than that, and in a subsequent chapter we shall have to see how this affects our theme. It is quite sufficient for our purpose if we have succeeded in showing that Paul, John, Matthew, and other writers of the New Testament, sought to present Jesus as the revelation of God's *ḥesed* and *'emeth*.

A Christology that is not based on the historical Jesus has most insecure foundations; we must therefore ask the question: does the revelation of God as *ḥesed* and *'emeth* form part of Jesus' own teaching and conscious vocation? In fact we have already found the beginning of an answer to this question in Matt. 23.23. But we must now attempt to give a fuller answer.

In the present state of Synoptic studies, he who claims that *any* element in the teaching attributed to Jesus in the Gospels is authentic proves himself thereby willing to rush in where angels fear to tread.[22] But Christology cannot maintain itself for long on the basis of complete agnosticism about the historical Jesus. I can only put down what I believe his teaching was. It is not a purely personal selection and can appeal to good authority.[23]

Jesus taught that in the prevailing emergency men can only hope to approach God in humility, penitence, and faith, and not on the basis of their complete observance of the Torah. The emergency was the last great crisis, the breaking in of the kingdom of God, which was to be ushered in by Jesus' own death and subsequent vindication. Of this we shall have more to say later. For the moment it is enough to note those passages in which emphasis is laid on the need for penitence in man's approach to God. We think of Mark 2.17:

> I came not to call the righteous, but sinners.

Luke 5.32 adds 'to repentance', no doubt a correct gloss. Does this mean that in Jesus' view there was an actual class of people who could be described as being righteous in God's eyes? It seems most unlikely. It is more in accordance with the rest of Jesus' teaching to suppose that in fact there were no righteous. The greatest error one could make was to imagine that one was righteous. This is surely confirmed by the parable of the labourers in the vineyard in Matt. 20.1–16. God gives what appears to be an unfair wage; but this is because there are no wages. All is of grace; all are equally in need of God's help. With this we can put three passages from Luke's Gospel. The first is the parable of the Pharisee and the publican in Luke 18.9–14; it is the publican who is commended (Luke actually uses the word 'justified'), the man who admits his bankruptcy in God's presence. Next comes Luke 17.7–10, the parable that gives us a vivid picture of the small farmer and his slave. Does the farmer thank the servant because he has done what was commanded? Of course not. But the relation of the slave to the farmer is exactly our relation to God.[24] We cannot claim any merit account with God. Thirdly there is the account of Jesus' reaction to the two instances of apparently unmerited suffering in Luke 13.1–5:

> Do you think that these Galileans were worse sinners than all the other Galileans because they suffered this? No; but unless you repent you will all likewise perish.

All men are brought under judgement by the imminent approach of the kingdom. All are equally guilty; therefore the only possible approach to God lies in an appeal to his mercy.

We may legitimately claim that this element of 'justification by faith' is not confined to any one source in the Synoptic tradition. We have found it in Mark, in Luke's special source, and in Matthew's special source. It is not therefore to be attributed to the peculiar outlook of any one of the Synoptic evangelists. We may confidently assert that it is an authentic part of Jesus' own teaching. Indeed we may also claim that Jesus exemplified his reliance on God's mercy in his own life. He taught his disciples to pray 'Our Father', and he used the very intimate term 'Abba' in his own prayers. He too approached God in faith, relying on God's mercy and not on any claim to have fulfilled the Torah to the letter.

Our one approach to God, then, is to come in faith, making no claim for ourselves and hoping for his mercy. But this hope, according to Jesus' teaching, is not vain. God is a God of mercy. Indeed, we do not need to take the initiative since God has already approached us. This is clearly brought out in the two parables of the lost sheep and the lost coin, and also in the parable of the prodigal son. God himself comes to seek those in Israel who are lost. This element is very prominent in Luke's special source, but we can find the same theme in Q and in Matthew's special material.[25] The Q source provides us with Matthew 5.44–5:

> But I say to you, Love your enemies and pray for those who persecute you, so that you may be sons of your Father who is in heaven; for he makes his sun rise on the evil and on the good, and sends rain on the just and on the unjust.

Luke's version is more specific in the epithets which it applies to God:

> he is kind to the ungrateful and the selfish. Be merciful even as your Father is merciful.

This is from Luke 6.35–6. The word translated 'kind' is *khrēstos* (cf. Wisd. 15.1 quoted above) and 'merciful' renders *oiktirmōn*. Perhaps Matthew's fifth beatitude, found in Matt. 5.7, could be compared with this:

> Blessed are the merciful, for they shall obtain mercy.

The word for 'merciful' is *eleēmōn*.

In both Matthew and Luke we find parables which emphasize God's readiness to forgive, and this is coupled with his requirement of love. In Matt. 18.23-35 there is the parable of the unforgiving servant. The point of the parable is no doubt that men should forgive one another, but this demand depends on the belief that God is also forgiving to the utmost.[26] The same moral is to be found in Luke's story of the two debtors, a tiny parable encapsulated within the story of the prostitute who approached Jesus when he was at Simon's house, Luke 7.36-50. The debtor who has been forgiven a greater debt will love the creditor more. As in Matthew's parable, the emphasis is on the requirement of love but behind lies the assumption that God is infinitely loving.

There is therefore evidence that the love and mercy of God formed an essential part of Jesus' teaching. God's mercy in fact was intimately connected with the coming of the kingdom, because only if he was infinitely merciful was the coming of the kingdom anything but a disaster. The advent of the kingdom performed in Jesus' teaching much the same office that the law performs in Paul's teaching: it drove all men back upon the mercy of God. Perhaps we may also say that the faithfulness of God is implicit in Jesus' teaching. He held, it seems, that God is *infinitely* merciful. Here the author of I Timothy is entirely true to the message of his master: there is no limit to the mercy of God displayed in Jesus Christ. This is not to suggest that Jesus understood the *ḥesed* and *'emeth* of God to be revealed in his own life in exactly the same way that the evangelists and Paul did. This is more than we have any right to expect. But we can confidently maintain that Jesus moved the mercy of God into the centre of the picture. He connected it integrally with the coming of the kingdom and he demonstrated in his own life and death a complete trust in God's mercy. This is an adequate basis for a Christology which understands Jesus Christ as the unique revelation of God's nature.

We may hope by this point to have laid the foundation for our doctrine of the incarnation. In Jesus Christ we can apprehend the revelation of God's essential nature as mercy and faithfulness, grace and truth in the Johannine sense. We have traced these two characteristics (or one determining attitude) of God through from the earliest traditions of Judaism down into the New Testament itself, where Jesus Christ is recognized by all major theological traditions as the supreme revelation of God's nature; and where the infinite mercy of God is a central element in Jesus' own teaching. We say 'recognized' deliberately, because this is essentially a process of recognition. Without the prior knowledge of the God of Israel the earliest disciples could not have recognized in Jesus the *ḥesed* and *'emeth* of God. We should also point out that, with one all-important exception, the process of recognizing God in Christ as far as we have traced it so far does not necessarily involve the acknowledgement of any superhuman element. The exception is, of course, Christ's resurrection, which was for Paul and John an essential part of his manifestation of God's mercy. But apart from this (and we devote proper attention to this later), the revelation of God's very nature in Jesus Christ has been understood in completely human terms, though not of course without a reference to the process whereby God made himself known to Israel of old, where indeed the human and superhuman cannot be always clearly distinguished.

It is also to be noted that our doctrine of the incarnation is heavily dependent on the concept of revelation. This is a mode of thought which gives great trouble to many philosophers of religion today, but we venture to suggest that in fact the theologian who is to be faithful to the Scriptures cannot dispense with it. Though words explicitly expressing the concept 'revelation' are relatively few in the New Testament, the belief that God can and does make himself known to man is absolutely fundamental to it, as material presented in this chapter alone should indicate. Because God is personal, it is entirely appropriate that he should be supremely revealed in a human person, Jesus Christ. The revelation of God as mercy and faithfulness in Jesus Christ confirms and realizes the knowledge of God as personal which Israel had gained in the course of more than a thousand years of history. That knowledge came in a great variety of modes (see Heb. 1.1), but behind it all the personal God was always known as present. Indeed the fact that God is personal in itself implies that he must reveal himself to men, since it seems to be the essence of persons to reveal themselves, not to be known immediately or objectively.[27]

2

THE DIVINITY REVEALED IN
THE HUMANITY

————◆••◆◆————

Karl Barth once wrote: 'In Jesus Christ . . . God activates and
proves his Godhead by the fact that he gives himself to the
suffering and limitation of the human creature.'[1] Barth himself
does not pursue this theme very far. It is the main purpose of this
chapter to show that this theme is to be found in Paul, in John,
and in Hebrews. The connection with the contents of the last
chapter should be clear enough: in the life of Jesus Christ we see
the mercy and the faithfulness of God supremely revealed. We
now consider the presentation of the self-giving love of God as
supremely revealed in the cross of Jesus Christ, an event in which
there was no superhuman element at all. Thus the essence of the
divinity is revealed in that which is completely human.

1

This theme is amply illustrated in the writings of St Paul. We
shall be chiefly occupied with three passages or groups of passages.
The first is Phil. 2.5–11, a passage on which probably more ink
has been spilt than on any other set of seven verses in the Epistles.
However, we do not propose to enter into detailed exegesis, but
merely to point out an interpretation of a phrase in verse 6 which
has recently been advocated by Professor C. F. D. Moule. The
phrase is:

> who, though he was in the form of God, did not count
> equality with God a thing to be grasped . . .

We have reproduced the RSV rendering though the whole point
of Moule's exegesis is to suggest that this is a mistaken translation.

All turns on the meaning of the word rendered 'a thing to be grasped', *harpagmos* in Greek. Moule argues that if we retain what would seem to be the natural meaning of the word in secular Greek 'the act of grasping', we can make good sense of it in the context.[2] He paraphrases the sentence thus on p. 274 of his article: 'Jesus did not reckon equality with God in terms of snatching,' and describes it as 'a revolutionary comment upon the world's values'. In a later article he expounds the significance of this for the doctrine of the incarnation thus: 'Jesus saw God-likeness essentially as giving and spending oneself out.'[3] If this interpretation were to be accepted, it would fit remarkably well with the concept of the divinity as manifested in the humanity. Paul is certainly making a revolutionary claim, for he is saying that divinity (not just 'God-likeness' but divine status) does not consist in privilege but in self-giving. From this it follows that the whole presupposition of the Kenotic school of theologians (based of course on this passage) was mistaken. Strictly speaking there can be no question of divine self-emptying, because divinity is most clearly manifested in self-giving and that must mean human self-giving. Professor Moule is inclined to doubt whether *doulos* in verse 7 ('taking the form of a *servant*') refers to the servant of the Lord in Isa. 53; but there is still the very illuminating suggestion made by J. Jeremias that *heauton ekenōsen* ('but he emptied himself') in the same verse is a translation of the phrase in Isa. 53.12 rendered by the RSV 'he poured out his soul'.[4] This leads to all sorts of valuable insights, some of which we shall pursue in the next chapter.[5] If obedience to God is the great medium of the revelation of God's nature, then surely the servant of the Lord, who was apparently obedient unto death, must be in some sense a means of revelation also. At any rate, if Moule's interpretation is correct, the main point of Paul's contention here is that divinity is supremely manifested in human self-giving, in fact in the human self-giving of Christ.[6]

Stählin makes the remark that in Paul *astheneia* ('weakness') can mean 'the point of revelation for divine *dunamis* ("power")'.[7] This may well be taken as the keynote of the next passage we are to study, I Cor. 1.18–31. The whole passage deserves quotation, but we can confine ourselves to verses 22–5:

For Jews demand signs and Greeks seek wisdom, but we preach Christ crucified, a stumbling block to Jews and folly to Gentiles, but to those who are called, both Jews and Greeks, Christ the power of God and the wisdom of God. For the foolishness of God is wiser than men, and the weakness of God is stronger than men.

Here is a magnificent exposition of the weakness and foolishness of God as manifested in his design which culminated in the cross and resurrection. What scandalized the Jews was the claim that the power of God (and hence his nature) is to be seen supremely in the complete human weakness of the cross. The opposite of the divine foolishness is human wisdom, presumably some sort of Gnostic or proto-Gnostic cosmology. The opposite of divine weakness is 'signs' (the same word as John uses, *sēmeia*). Presumably this means a Messiah accredited by undeniable miracles, just the sort of sign which Jesus repudiated. We should also observe that integrally connected with the apprehension of the divine revelation is the concept of 'boasting'. In its wrong sense boasting seems to mean reliance on anything whatever, no matter how sacred and venerable, except the action of God in Christ. But there is a right kind of boasting which is very much the same as justification by faith. The passage we are considering ends with the words in verse 31:

therefore, as it is written, 'Let him who boasts, boast of the Lord.'

We should note a slight inaccuracy in the RSV. A more accurate rendering of the citation from Jeremiah is:

'Let him who boasts, boast in the Lord.

'The Lord' is of course Christ and Paul is here finding in Scripture his doctrine of Christians being 'in Christ'. Goudge well quotes Bengel: 'Not before him, but in him can we glory.'[8] Here then is a clear statement from Paul that the action of God is manifested at the point where Jesus is most obviously human, with specific emphasis on the fact that there is nothing miraculous, in the sense of superhuman, about the medium of revelation.

The citation of Jer. 9.24 also occurs in 2 Cor. 10.17, and this

c

citation introduces us to Paul's use of 'weakness' to indicate a situation in which God's power is manifested in human weakness or inadequacy. It would be a distraction from our main theme to give full account of Paul's concept of weakness. Indeed it would involve giving something like a commentary on 2 Corinthians, for this is a subject which appears frequently in that Epistle. But we must notice some instances of its occurrence, since the power of God manifested in human weakness is integrally connected with the theme of God's nature manifested in humanity. One outstanding example of this usage occurs not in 2 Corinthians but in 1 Cor. 4.8–13. Paul is contrasting the 'spectator' attitude of the Corinthians with the strenuous and perilous life lived by himself and his fellow-workers in the gospel. He draws a series of ironical contrasts between the security of the Corinthians and the precarious situation of the apostles. Throughout the passage the description of the apostles' life might very well be a description of the life of Christ. In 4.10 he writes:

> We are fools for Christ's sake, but you are wise in Christ. We are weak but you are strong. You are held in honour, but we in disrepute.

Here is that 'foolishness' and 'weakness' which we have already met in 1.25 attributed to God in Christ. The passage ends in verse 13 with the words:

> we have become, and are now, as the refuse of the world, the offscouring of all things.

The words translated 'refuse' and 'offscouring' (*perikatharmata* and *peripsēma* respectively) bear a strong expiatory or propitiatory meaning in both scriptural and secular Greek. The reference to God's act of expiation in Christ can hardly be denied. Here then is God's action revealed in the very weakness of obedient humanity.

We now return to 2 Corinthians. In chapters 10—13 Paul is defending himself passionately against a series of damaging accusations that have been levelled against him by the opposition party. In chapter 11 he allows himself to boast in what he considers the wrong sense, that is to boast of his own achievements and experiences. But by the end of the chapter he has repudiated this line of argument, and in 11.30 he writes:

> If I must boast, I will boast of the things that show my weakness.

He goes on to refer to an adventure that befell him in Damascus, when he had to be lowered out of a window in a basket in order to avoid the deputy of King Aretas. Allo is no doubt right here in saying that Paul in narrating this incident wants to show that he was not always cast in the role of hero.[9] The tenth verse of the next chapter seems to interpret the sense in which we are to understand Paul here.

> For the sake of Christ, then, I am content with weaknesses, insults, hardships, persecutions, and calamities; for when I am weak, then I am strong.

This comment actually comes after a reference to the mysterious 'thorn in the flesh' (12.7). We need not go into the much discussed question as to what this meant,[10] but we may well quote Paul's conclusion about it (12.8–9):

> Three times I besought the Lord about this, that it should leave me; but he said to me, 'My grace is sufficient for you, for my power is made perfect in weakness.' I will all the more gladly boast of my weaknesses, that the power of Christ may rest upon me.

Editors have emphasized the significance of the word translated 'rest upon' here, *episkēnōsē/i*. It is unique here in the New Testament, and recalls the *eskēnōsen* ('*dwelt* among us') of John 1.14. This word or cognates are frequently used in the Septuagint to translate words for the divine indwelling. R. P. C. Hanson comments: 'The Christian Church is now the place where God rests temporarily between the cross and the end.'[11] Héring notes that in Judaism the *Shekinah* was often said to rest upon the elect. But for Paul Christ is the *Shekinah* or divine manifestation. The fact that this presence is manifested in human weakness is therefore immensely significant.

Paul sums up his argument in 13.1–4 and warns his readers that the weakness in which Christ's power is displayed is not an ineffective weakness; in verse 4 he writes of Christ:

For he was crucified in weakness, but lives by the power of
God. For we are weak in him, but in dealing with you we shall
live with him by the power of God.

We may explain these words thus: Paul is weak in Christ, i.e. all
his power comes from Christ, not from himself. Christ was
crucified 'in weakness', i.e. as man all his power was ascribed to
God not to himself and he made no effort to save himself from the
cross which was God's will for him. But he lives from the power
of God, manifested in the resurrection. This does not merely
mean: 'Christ was weak by worldly standards because he trusted
in God alone; thanks to the resurrection he is now strong.' It
means that the weakness shown in the crucifixion is really divine
strength. The secret is manifested in the resurrection and in the
living Christ today apprehended by faith. The clue is self-giving.
So this is not an eschatological hope of Paul's. Paul is always weak
in Christ, i.e. giving himself (in Christ) for the benefit of his
converts. The power of God will be shown when the Corinthians
come to understand this and to live the same sort of life. This is
essentially the same message as that which we meet in 1 Cor.
4.8–13. Strachan rightly concludes apropos this passage that the
power of Christ and the weakness of Christ are identical;[12] and
R. P. C. Hanson comments: 'He [Paul] falls back for his authority
simply in the fact that the weakness of Christ is reproduced in
him.' Thus the theme of the divine nature revealed in the very
humanness of the humanity of Christ is one which is not only
applied by Paul to Christ but is also worked out in the life of
Christ as reproduced in the lives of his disciples.

2

The same theme of the divinity manifested in the humanity meets
us in the Fourth Gospel. We may perhaps approach the subject
by considering a question which Käsemann asks: what, he
inquires, is the content of the prophetic word which is uttered in
the Word made flesh?[13] He answers that it is the witness of the
divinity of the Logos. We would suggest that Käsemann has not
given sufficient attention to John 1.1–18 in this context. It is true
that according to the Fourth Gospel the ontological unity of the

Father and the Son is disclosed in Jesus' career. But this is not the ultimate: the reason for emphasizing this unity is that we should be assured that it really is God whom we encounter in this career. And in this part of the prologue John states emphatically what is the nature of that God who is revealed through Christ: he is God full of grace and truth. What is ultimately revealed in Christ is God's authentic nature. Thus John's picture of Jesus does not give us a situation in which, as Käsemann suggests, the divine only condescends to the temporal to the minimum extent necessary for saving contact; on the contrary the Gospel represents the full reality, humiliation, and weakness of the incarnation as being essential for the full revelation of God's nature. We reach the final paradox when we claim, as we may, that John, whose portrait of Jesus seems farthest from actual history, is of all the evangelists the most insistent that the flesh is the place where the full revelation has taken place.

But is this emphasis maintained throughout the Gospel? Might it not be that the prologue states a position from which the rest of the Gospel tends to fall away? This suggestion is not borne out by the use of the word *doxa* ('glory') and cognates in the Gospel. It has often been pointed out that in the Fourth Gospel that word frequently refers to the cross. Thus in 12.23 Jesus says:

The hour has come for the Son of Man to be glorified (*doxasthē/i*).

He goes on in the ensuing verses to speak of his death. Immediately afterwards comes what many scholars believe to be John's version of Gethsemane, where Jesus' prayer is: 'Father, glorify thy name'. In the context this can only mean that Jesus accepts the destiny of the cross. The same meaning is found in 7.18–19, where seeking the Father's glory involves Jesus being killed by the Jews. This theme reaches its climax in 17.1–5, where the prayer 'glorify thy Son' means in effect 'accept my offering of myself in death'. The origin of this remarkable use of *doxa* and cognates is no doubt to be found in the Septuagint translation of Isa. 52.13. The RSV runs:

Behold my servant shall prosper,
  he shall be exalted and lifted up,
  and shall be very high.

The Septuagint has used *hypsōthēsetai* and *doxasthēsetai* to render the last three verbs in this sentence. Connected with this is John's use of *hupsoun* 'to lift up' or 'exalt' in 3.14; 8.28; 12.32. In all these passages the verb is used in a double sense. It means both 'to be exalted' and 'to be raised from the ground on the cross'. It is characteristic of the Johannine irony that what means one thing to outsiders means something else also to believers. Thus according to John Jesus is most highly exalted when he is apparently most deeply degraded; and God's glory, for those who have eyes of faith, shines most clearly at the moment when Jesus dies on the cross in weakness and in totally human humiliation. At this point John's message coincides exactly with Paul's in such passages as 1 Cor. 1.18-31. It is true indeed that behind the cross lies the resurrection, and both the glory and the lifting up are incomplete without this. But John makes it quite plain that the glory does not first become manifest at the resurrection: it is to be seen on the cross, and supremely there. Thus John unmistakably and perhaps surprisingly asserts that God's nature is supremely revealed in the completely human death of Christ. The divinity becomes clearest at the very point where Jesus would seem to be most disastrously human.

But what of Jesus' miracles, which John, like the other evangelists, goes out of his way to record? Do they not count against the suggestion that for John God was revealed in the humanness of Christ's humanity? A consideration of the miracles as narrated in the Fourth Gospel is certainly in order here. One could say of Jesus' miracles in the Synoptic Gospels that they are indications of the presence of God in Jesus; they are skirmishes and engagements in the struggle between God and Satan, episodes that cause amazement and make men ask, who is this? They are called *dunameis*, acts of power. Except for the word *dunameis*, which John never uses, all this is equally true of the miracles in John's Gospel. But much more can be said about them. In the Fourth Gospel the miracles of Jesus are carefully selected and schematized. Jesus is never represented as healing people promiscuously, as he is sometimes in the Synoptic Gospels. And John uses a special word for the miracles; he calls them *sēmeia*, 'signs'. It is widely agreed that John wishes to relate seven such signs, though there is much less agreement as to which exactly those seven are. In particular there is doubt as to whether the cross and resurrection is the seventh and culminative sign, as C. H. Dodd holds. It is in favour of this view that the actual event of the resurrection is not described, and that it therefore shares in the element of hiddenness which belongs to nearly all the signs. Also in John's Gospel alone is Jesus regarded as bringing about his resurrection himself (see 10.17–18). Thus, if the cross and resurrection is the last sign, it is, like the rest, brought about by Jesus himself.

We have mentioned a certain hiddenness about the signs, or at least about most of them. We do not normally see them taking place: at Cana we see the result of the miracle, the water which has been turned into wine, but not the actual change taking place. In 4.46–54 the official's son is cured at long range; we do not witness the cure. In 9.7 the blind man goes off to the pool of Siloam and comes back seeing; we do not witness the actual restoration of sight. In chapter 6 we do not have an actual description of the multiplication of the loaves (though it must be said that this feature is common to all four accounts of the miracle). In the narrative of the raising of Lazarus we are not permitted to see the dead man in the act of coming to life; we see him issue from the tomb. Is the reason for this hiddenness perhaps connected with the fact that in John the signs are not exactly what Käsemann claims they are, 'proofs of the divine power in the sphere of the transitory'?[14]

It is interesting to observe that John, in common with the other evangelists, records Jesus' refusal to give a sign; see 2.18; 6.30. To be absolutely exact, Jesus is not represented as outrightly refusing so much as answering the challenge ambiguously. In chapter 2 he offers the sign of his own death and resurrection; in chapter 6 (as I believe) he hints that he has already given the sign the Jews ask for, since he was the real source of the manna in the wilderness.[15] In John's scheme of things, therefore, there must be a sort of sign which is undesirable. Presumably this is the sort of superhuman miracle which nobody could mistake and which commands instant assent (see above our remarks on 1 Cor. 1.22). Does this not imply that the sort of sign which Jesus did supply in abundance still required faith in order to understand it? If so, 'proofs' is hardly the right word for the signs. Or rather, it depends on what you mean by proofs. It is true that later Christian apologetic tradition proceeded to use Jesus' miracles as proofs of his divinity, sometimes in the most mechanical manner; but this is not evidence that John meant to use them thus.

Perhaps it might be useful at this point to ask, of what are the 'signs' signs? We get a specific answer in 2.11, where we are told that the first sign performed by Jesus 'manifested his glory'. This should put us on the alert: what the signs manifest is precisely what the cross manifests, the self-giving nature of God. And this is something which can never be demonstratively proved; it always needs faith to understand it. So a better description of the signs than the word 'proofs' is perhaps this: the signs provide the right milieu for belief. In the Fourth Gospel John intimates that it is possible to believe the signs and yet to fail to reach full and satisfactory faith; see 4.48; 10.41–2; 12.37. Schnackenburg well writes of the signs 'they only disclose their meaning when they are greeted with faith'.[16] He adds that Jesus himself is the greatest sign. Could we perhaps say that the signs are in the historical life of Jesus what the sacraments are in the life of the Church, opportunities for faith in which the nature and action of God may be grasped by faith?

Thus Käsemann would seem to be wide of the mark when he writes: 'No Christian at the end of the first century could have come to the idea that God could enter the human scene without miracles.'[17] The miracles in the Fourth Gospel subserve the purpose of revelation, to show that God is abounding in steadfast love and faithfulness. They are not used as superhuman marvels to prove God's presence. Käsemann's further suggestion that the miraculous element in the signs is played up by John in order to enhance Jesus' glory is not borne out by the evidence. Käsemann would point to such passages as 9.3 and 11.4. In the first the birth of the blind man is described as taking place in order that the works of God might be manifested in him. In the second Lazarus' illness is stated to be

> for the glory of God, so that the Son of God may be glorified by means of it.

As far as 9.3 is concerned, the manifesting of the works of God means the manifesting of God's self-giving love; the miraculous element is part of this, but not the main part. Jesus heals the man for the love of God, not in order to demonstrate God's marvellous power. The same thing might be said about 11.4; but here we can detect another feature: the glorifying of the Son of God means his death. John represents the raising of Lazarus as the immediate cause of the plot against Jesus' life formed by the Jewish authorities. This miracle is therefore part of God's design whereby the Son of Man must die. In short, the signs in the Fourth Gospel, despite the miraculous element in them, fall into the main pattern of revelation: God full of grace and truth is shown in the Word made flesh, and the flesh is the essential and indispensable medium of revelation.

We must now approach the same theme in John from a different point of view; this is the use of the word 'name' in connection with God and how it relates to the Father's love for the Son. Our aim will be to show that what the Father's name means is God's nature as mercy and faithfulness; and secondly that the Father's love for the Son, in so far as it presents a model for Christians to follow, means the relation between God and the historical Jesus, and that this relation also reveals primarily God's nature as love rather than the ontological relationship between God and the Word. The relevance to our theme is that, if these claims can be made good, here is another way in which the historical Jesus is seen as the revelation of God's nature; and here also the relationship of the human Jesus to God is the medium of revelation. Thus here also the very humanity is essential to the revelation.

We are only concerned with those passages in the Fourth Gospel where the name of God indicates the revelation of God; we can put on one side places where the name has some other connotation, such as 1.12 or 3.18. We begin with 5.42–3:

> But I know that you have not the love of God within you. I have come in my Father's name, and you do not receive me.

This is taken by a great many editors to mean that the Son has come in the Father's authority, and that it is therefore not connected with the revelation of God. But a number of editors realize that the thought of revelation cannot be excluded. Thus Westcott writes: 'The glory of the Messiah lies in his perfect fellowship with the Father,' and he glosses 'in the name' with 'revealing God to you in this character'.[18] Bernard describes the name as 'the revelation of the Being of God'. This is a passage where the two themes come together, revelation of the Father and the significance of love: if men had had love towards God, they would have recognized in Jesus the Father's love.

The next passage is 10.25, where Jesus says:

> The works that I do in my Father's name, they bear witness to me.

This must mean revelation, since it is uttered in response to a challenge from the Jews to declare whether he is the Christ. He calls his works to witness, not merely that he is the Christ, but that he comes in his Father's name. In other words, in the Son's works the Jews can recognize the Father's revelation.

In 12.28, at what is probably John's account of the Gethsemane experience, Jesus prays:

> Father, glorify thy name.

The phrase is no doubt a conscious echo of the Lord's Prayer, but it is equally clear that here the glorifying of the name means the revelation of God's nature in the cross and resurrection. Editors are pretty well unanimous on this point.[19] Bultmann's comment is worth quoting: 'If the Father glorifies himself (that is reveals himself) through the Son's activity, the Son is likewise glorified as the revealer.' Equally clear is 14.26, where the Paraclete is one whom the Father will send in Jesus' name. His function is teaching, so the name must imply revelation—though this does not of course apply to the period of the incarnation.

We now reach the great high-priestly prayers in chapter 17, where our two themes, revelation and love, most obviously meet. The connection is made clear in verse 11, where Jesus prays:

> Holy Father, keep them in thy name, which thou hast given me, that they may be one, even as we are one.

Here we encounter the mysterious suggestion that the unity of the Father and the Son is an example or model for the unity of Christians with each other, and (in verse 21) for the unity of Christians with Christ. It is associated with the name, which means the revealed nature of God. The revelatory significance of the name is integral here, since the unity is held up as a model.

The question is this: does John actually expect Christians to model their unity (moral and spiritual) on the ontological unity which has existed between the Father and the Son from all eternity? It seems unlikely, indeed unreasonable. How can Christians be expected to strive for a unity which they must by God's help achieve under the inspiration of a metaphysical unity which is eternal and indissoluble? Surely a much more realistic model would be a unity that is itself moral and spiritual, the obedience which the historical Jesus exhibited to the Father? But some editors do in fact conclude that it is the precosmic unity that is meant here. Thus Westcott writes: 'As the divine unity consists with a variety of Persons, so too the final unity of men does not exclude but perfectly harmonises the separate being of each in the whole'—a confusion of 'Person' as used in trinitarian theology with 'person' as used in modern psychology that would seem disastrous for the former. But Westcott plunges still deeper; commenting on verses 20-4, he writes that the unity of believers is 'a vital unity . . . far more than a mere moral unity of purpose, feeling, affection'. No doubt such language was easier in the idealistic philosophical atmosphere which prevailed in the Victorian era. C. K. Barrett takes the same view: the Father and the Son, he says, are one and yet distinct; so believers are to be 'distinct from God, yet abiding in God'.[20] But, if the relation of believers to God is to be in the same category as the relation of the Son to the Father from all eternity, then John is committed to a thoroughgoing Monism of which any Indian philosopher might be proud. It is a pity that a very recent work by a distinguished Christian philosopher should be committed to exactly the same view. Dr Helen Oppenheimer writes: 'The bond of unity between ourselves and God is the very same as the bond of unity within God himself.'[21] This rash and unnecessary conclusion from the seventeenth chapter of the Fourth Gospel is, I believe, no small part of the reason why Dr Oppenheimer finds herself in almost insuperable difficulties when she tries to define the nature of the unity that existed between the Word and the Jesus of history.

Others, however, are more cautious, and suggest that the unity which is to be a model for Christians is the unity of the incarnate Son with the Father. Marsh's comment is interesting: 'the only unity possible between the Father and the incarnate Son is that between one who suffers and who is all-glorious. This unity the Church is to share.'[22] We should note also Karl Rahner's warning that it is dangerous to infer 'the eternal generation of the Logos' from Jesus' historical relation to the Father.[23] We thus have something like a three-tier system in John's thought: the revelation of the divine name is the revelation of God as full of grace and truth. This revelation is made by means of the Son's obedience to the Father in his incarnate life. The members of the Church in their turn manifest this to the world by their mutual love.

This theme is made absolutely explicit in verses 21–3:

> . . . that they may all be one; even as thou, Father, art in me and I in thee, that they also may be in us, so that the world may believe that thou hast sent me. The glory which thou hast given me I have given to them, that they may be one even as we are one, I in them and thou in me, that they may become perfectly one, so that the world may know that thou hast sent me and hast loved them even as thou hast loved me.

In each case the past or perfect tense ('which thou hast given me', 'thou hast sent me') must refer to the incarnate life and not to the eternal relationship between the Father and the Son. Thus God's nature can only be manifested, and reproduced in Christians, because of the human life of Jesus Christ. Lagrange is surely right when he says that the glory in this passage is not the glory of the uncreate Son of God. God never *gave* him that; it was his by right. It is the glory of the Son of God incarnate which was reflected on the human nature.[24] It is true that the very next verse refers to 'my glory which thou hast given me in thy love for me before the beginning of the world'. But this does not form part of the revelation. Christians only hope to see this beyond this world, when they are with Christ where he is.

The last verse of chapter 17 connects the revelation with the Father's love more clearly than ever:

> I made known to them thy name and I will make it known, that the love with which thou hast loved me may be in them, and I in them.

Christians, then, are to reflect the love of the Father to the Son. Does this mean that they are to reflect the bond which exists between the Father and the Word from all eternity? Not necessarily. In fact an inspection of the other places in the Gospel where the Father's love for the Son is mentioned suggests the reverse. Thus in 3.35 we read:

> the Father loves the Son and has given all things into his hand.

This must refer to the incarnate life. So also in 10.17:

> For this reason the Father loves me, because I lay down my life, that I may take it again.

Nothing could be more explicit: the Father's love is integrally connected with the cross and resurrection. In 14.31 we read:

> but I do as the Father has commanded me, so that the world may know that I love the Father.

Here is the mutual love: the Son's love for the Father is revealed in his obedience. Finally we note 15.9-10:

> As the Father has loved me, so have I loved you; abide in my love. If you keep my commandments, you will abide in my love, just as I have kept my Father's commandments and abide in his love.

The Son represents perfectly obedient humanity; he therefore also represents the perfect relationship between God and man. The love which the disciples are to reproduce is the human love of the Son for the Father, expressed in his human obedience in keeping the Father's commandments.

We may express in a few sentences the significance for our theme of this discussion of the Father's name and the Father's love. The conclusions we draw are as follows:

(*a*) The revelation of God's name means the revelation of God as grace (mercy, love) and truth (faithfulness).

(*b*) Since the love, in as far as it is a model for Christians, indicates the human relationship of the Son to the Father, that relationship reveals to us primarily God as full of love and truth, and not (primarily at least) the ontological relationship of God to the Word.

(c) The relevance of all this to our theme is that here too the revelation of God's nature is made through the humanity and that therefore the humanity is the essential and indispensable medium for the revelation of the nature of God. Thus we find ourselves in complete disagreement with Käsemann when he says that Jesus' obedience in the Fourth Gospel should not be interpreted 'moralistically'.[25] If there is no moral element in Jesus' obedience, how can it be a model for believers? Much more in accordance with John's thought is Cadman's insistence (indeed it is the one great virtue of an otherwise rather disappointing book) that Jesus' obedience to the Father's commands, and his requirement that the disciples should obey in the same way, shows that what is in question is Jesus' human obedience and not any notion of his automatically carrying out a 'blueprint' received in heaven.[26]

3

We have in this chapter attempted to show that both Paul and John, though they do not use an identical Christology, regard the humanness of Jesus Christ as the essential medium whereby the nature of God as self-giving love has been revealed. It is essential in the sense that the revelation could have been made in no other way. The nature of God is manifested in the complete humanity of Jesus Christ in a way which could not have been accomplished by some superhuman manifestation. One question might well occur at this point: what about the third major theological tradition in the New Testament, the Epistle to the Hebrews? Can we find the same theme there?

We do not have the space to explore the question fully, but I believe we can find this theme in Hebrews. In the opening verses of the Epistle the author sets out his Christology in the highest terms. God:

> has spoken to us by a Son, whom he appointed the heir of all things, through whom also he created the world. He reflects the glory of God and bears the very stamp of his nature, upholding the universe by his word of power.

In the rest of the chapter the author demonstrates by means of scriptural quotations that the Son is higher than any of the angels and that the Father addresses him as God (Heb. 1.8). There can be no doubt that the author held a very high Christology indeed.

We have quoted the RSV, which translates 1.3 with 'He reflects the glory of God and bears the very stamp of his nature.' But these verbs in the RSV translate nouns in the Greek. Let us take a more literal translation: 'being the reflection (*apaugasma*) of God's glory and the stamp (*kharaktēr*) of his nature'. Both these indicate that the Son perfectly reflects God's nature. We need not here ask how this could be known in the Son's pre-existent state; but we may very pertinently ask how the historical Jesus according to the author of Hebrews manifested God's nature, reflected God's glory? Very remarkably, the author of Hebrews gives a much more explicit answer to this question than Paul does. We turn to Heb. 5.7–10:

> In the days of his flesh Jesus offered up prayers and supplications, with loud cries and tears, to him who was able to save him from death, and he was heard for his godly fear.[27] Although he was a Son, he learned obedience through what he suffered; and being made perfect he became the source of eternal salvation to all who obey him, being designated by God a high priest after the order of Melchizedek.

Thus being the reflection and stamp of the Father's very nature must be compatible with a full humanity, a humanity which is actually described in terms of growth ('being made perfect') and of learning through suffering. The only conclusion that will make sense of the author's Christology is that the divine image is actually mediated by the process of 'learning obedience through what he suffered'. In other words, in the Epistle to the Hebrews also the author must have held that the divinity is manifested by means of the humanity. In the next chapter we shall have to consider in another context what it means to learn obedience through suffering. For the moment we may be content to note that the theme we are studying is implicit in the Epistle to the Hebrews.

4

One of the most important assumptions lying behind the New Testament exposition of the divinity as revealed in the humanity is the implication that man is *capax Dei*, that human nature is so designed as to be capable of revealing the Word, indeed uniquely capable of revealing him. This point is well urged by Karl Rahner; it comes in the context of his argument that incarnation in man is a mode of communication peculiar to the Word in the Holy Trinity. Human nature, he says, is specifically designed to reveal the Logos; it is not a mode which he just happened to choose; 'human nature is not a mask (the *prosōpon*) assumed from without, from behind which the Logos hides to act things out in the world. From the start it is the constitutive, real symbol of the Logos himself.'[28] The point is equally well made by Bultmann, commenting on John 1.14: 'But this is the paradox that runs all through the Gospel, that the *doxa* is not beside the flesh, or to be seen through the flesh as through a transparent medium, but nowhere else than *in* the flesh. . . . The revelation is thus there in a genuine veiling.'[29]

Is this what Charles Wesley meant in his famous Christmas hymn?

> Veiled in flesh the godhead see.

It is ambiguous, because it might suggest that the flesh constitutes an impediment to seeing the godhead, even perhaps Bultmann's 'transparent medium'. It cannot be denied that traditional Christology has tended to give this impression, if not to say so explicitly. The concept of Jesus as 'God incognito' is not at all far from the traditional view. Thus Ambrose can write as follows: 'He took on him that which he was not that he might hide that which was his',[30] which is certainly not what Paul and John are trying to convey about the incarnation. At a somewhat deeper level we might bring the same criticism to bear on the way in which, some hundred years later, Leo dealt with what theologians call the *communicatio idiomatum*, the arrangement whereby what is strictly speaking true of only one of Christ's two natures according to Chalcedonian Christology can also be predicated of the other. Leo writes: 'Each nature performs its proper functions in communion with the other; the Word performs what pertains to the Word, the flesh what pertains to the flesh. The one is resplendent with miracles, the other submits to insults.'[31] In other words, as Sellers paraphrases it, 'shame belonged to the Lord's manhood and glory to his Godhead' (p. 248). But this is not what Paul and John are saying: the glory belonged to the suffering humanity. Once distinguish the natures like this (or rather once express the problem in terms of two natures), and the cutting edge of the deepest message of the New Testament is blunted. Even the device of the *communicatio idiomatum* will not restore the original message.

This concept of a *deus incognitus*, God appearing incognito, has plenty of precedent in other religious traditions. One could point, for example, to the *Bhagavad Gītā*. Here Krishna, who is an epiphany (*avatār*) of Vishnu, lives on earth in the capacity of Arjuna's charioteer. The disguise is fairly thin, since Arjuna before battle consults Krishna as an authority on religion and morals; and the magnificent theophany in chapter XI does away with all disguise. More relevant perhaps is Euripides' great play *The Bacchae*. Dionysius visits the dominions of King Pentheus disguised as the leader of a band of enthusiasts. Pentheus meets him, objects to his presence, and throws him into prison. But the prison is smashed by an earthquake. Dionysius and his devotees escape to the mountains, and Pentheus is terribly punished. He is seized with a mad desire to spy upon the Dionysian celebrations: he disguises himself as a woman and joins the throng in the mountains. But the devotees, under the illusion that he is a lion, attack him, led by Pentheus' own mother Agave, and tear him to pieces. The contrast with the Christian doctrine of the incarnation could not be more poignant. In the Christian account God does indeed appear in a human life, but for him there is no escape and no theophany.[32] He is put to death by men without offering any resistance. If there is a punishment for this, it is one which the Jews bring on themselves and not one deliberately inflicted by God. Above all, the manifestation of God is to be apprehended (by faith) in the very act of his accepting a human existence, and supremely in the human death.

There is, however, one passage in Paul where Christ appears to be presented as God incognito, or at least where the humanity appears to be represented as hiding the divinity, and that is 1 Cor. 2.6–10, a passage continuous with one we discussed at the beginning of this chapter:

Grace and Truth

Yet among the mature we do impart wisdom, although it is not a wisdom of this age or of the rulers of this age, who are doomed to pass away. But we impart a secret and hidden wisdom of God, which God decreed before the ages for our glorification. None of the rulers of this age understood this; for if they had, they would not have crucified the Lord of glory. But, as it is written,

'What no eye has seen, nor ear heard,
nor the heart of man conceived,
what God has prepared for those who love him,'

God has revealed to us through the Spirit.

I have already commented on this passage elsewhere.[33] I was mainly concerned to show that in this passage Paul is writing a sort of midrash on Ps. 24 in the Septuagint. In that Psalm in the Greek version by a mistranslation the 'gates' who are to 'lift up their heads' become 'the rulers'. It was from that Psalm, I suggested, that Paul took the phrase 'the Lord of glory' (it appears there as 'the king of glory'); the Psalm spoke to him of the entry of the victorious Christ into heaven after conquering the demonic powers. The repeated question 'who is the king of glory?' shows that the powers had failed to recognize him. I quoted Justin, *Dialogue* 36.5–6, where very much this interpretation of Ps. 24 is put forward: 'For when the rulers of heaven saw that he had an unattractive, dishonoured, and inglorious appearance, not recognizing him, they asked: "Who is this king of glory?".' I drew the conclusion that the scriptural quotation in verse 9 does not refer to the joys of heaven or of the parousia, as most editors assume, but to the events of the cross and resurrection. For our purpose here it will be sufficient to note two points about Justin's treatment of Ps. 24: first, he is well aware of the traditional Jewish exegesis of the Psalm, that it belongs to the moment when Solomon was about to dedicate the temple; but he rejects it in favour of his own christological one.[34] Secondly, Justin claims that the powers failed to recognize the Lord of glory not specifically because of his human appearance, but because of his dishonoured appearance.

Our concern is to ask the question, why did the rulers fail to recognize the wisdom of God? But this is an obscure passage, so we cannot hope to answer this question until a number of other problems have been resolved. First, it is the 'world rulers', the demonic powers, of whom Paul is speaking. There are in fact two other interpretations of this phrase 'the rulers of this age' to be found in Christian tradition; either that it means the political rulers of Palestine—Caiaphas and Pilate; or that it means men of influence in the realm of culture—orators, poets, philosophers.[35] But virtually all modern editors accept that the phrase refers to the demonic powers.[36] Then Paul's quotation in verse 9 is full of problems; there is no absolute agreement as to where it comes from, though Isa. 64.4 does seem to be the most likely source. Paul quotes it in a form which is found neither in the Hebrew nor the Greek. On the other hand, both the Masoretic Text and the text of the Septuagint present difficulties. I can only state dogmatically that in my opinion Paul has not altered the text of the quotation to serve his purpose. At any rate all versions of the Isaiah quotation including the Targum are agreed that this is a passage about seeing God and about what God has promised for those who do see him. One other preliminary point must be made: Paul says that the rulers failed to recognize the wisdom of God. This means they failed to recognize God's design in Christ; but in effect it comes to the same thing as saying that they failed to recognize who Christ was. Though Paul is speaking here primarily in terms of God's act of salvation, the question of revelation cannot be avoided, as becomes clear whenever the passage is expounded in depth.

We may now revert to our question: why did the rulers fail to recognize the wisdom of God? Evans writes: 'They thought of Christ as a mere man, and so contrived what was intended to be his end but actually became the beginning of their own.'[37] This suggests that Paul held an essentially Chalcedonian Christology; the divinity was hidden by the humanity. But in verse 7 where Paul writes of 'the secret and hidden wisdom' he does not mean that the divinity was hidden by the humanity. On the contrary, on the cross the divinity is revealed by the humanity. Weiss makes the illuminating remark that the powers do not understand God's scheme because their disobedience has removed them far from God.[38] This is much nearer the mark: in order to recognize the divinity in the humanity faith is needed. But faith is impossible for those who are disobedient to God. The right account therefore seems to be that the powers failed to recognize the Lord of glory when he appeared as man. But it was not that the divinity lay hid behind the humanity, like the hook hidden in the bait in the famous patristic simile. Rather the powers failed to recognize that the humanity ('the weakness of God') revealed God's nature. We repeat that Paul puts it in soteriological terms: they failed to recognize God's wonderful design. But if you are to speak in terms of revelation, as you must, you have to say that they failed to recognize God's very nature revealed in the humanity of Christ.

It is remarkable that we have a sort of brief commentary on 1 Cor. 1.18—2.10 written within roughly sixty years of the appearance of 1 Corinthians. This is to be found in Ignatius' *Epistle to the Ephesians*, xvii–xix. It is very interesting from the point of view of our study because it seems to show the development of the traditional Christology which is being read into Paul's Christology. We quote from xvii.2 to the end of xix in J. B. Lightfoot's translation:[39]

> And wherefore do we not all walk prudently, receiving the knowledge of God, which is Jesus Christ? Why perish we in our folly, not knowing the gift of grace which the Lord hath truly sent? My spirit is made an offscouring for the Cross, which is a stumbling-block to them that are unbelievers, but to us salvation and life eternal. *Where is the wise? Where is the disputer?* Where is the boasting of them that are called prudent? For our God, Jesus the Christ, was conceived in the womb of Mary according to a dispensation, of the seed of David but also of the Holy Ghost; and he was born and was baptized that by his passion he might cleanse water. And hidden from the prince of this world were the virginity of Mary and her child-bearing and likewise also the death of the Lord—three mysteries to be cried aloud—the which were wrought in the silence of God. How then were they made manifest to the ages? A star shone forth in the heaven above all the stars. . . . From that time forward every sorcery and every spell was dissolved, the ignorance of wickedness vanished away, the ancient kingdom was pulled down, when God appeared in the likeness of man (*theou anthrōpinōs phaneroumenou*) unto *newness* of everlasting *life*; and that which had been perfected in the

counsels of God began to take effect. Thence all things were perturbed, because the abolishing of death was taken in hand.

There can be no doubt whatever that Ignatius has our passage in mind; there are too many cross-references to 1 Cor. 1.18—2.10 for there to be any uncertainty about this. It is interesting therefore to observe that Ignatius does understand 'the rulers of this age' as the demonic powers; but he subsumes them all under one ruler, as Paul does in 2 Cor. 4.4. Ignatius does however probably refer to them in the plural in XIX.2, where 'How then were they made manifest to the ages?' refers to the aeons, a Gnostic word for super-human powers. Moreover he makes it quite plain that these rulers are evil and that the incarnation and cross overcame their power. Next we should remark that Ignatius does understand this passage in terms of revelation, even though Paul's emphasis is on soteriology. And thirdly we note that Ignatius has applied to the whole life of Jesus, and especially to his birth, what Paul has said of his death only. This is perfectly legitimate, and indeed must follow from Paul's own assumptions. It so happens of course that Paul shows no knowledge of any events connected with Jesus' birth.

However, Ignatius' Christology does not seem to be quite the same as Paul's. Could Paul have written 'our God Jesus Christ was carried in Mary's womb' (this is the literal sense)? Here surely is the God-man of traditional Christology. Again, Ignatius seems to go out of his way to stress the miraculous elements in Jesus' life: his conception in the womb of a virgin is on an equal footing with his death in God's design. In a passage which we have omitted Ignatius elaborates the extraordinary nature of the star of Bethlehem and the astonishment which it produced. Above all, that phrase *theou anthrōpinōs phaneroumenou* ('when God appeared in the likeness of man') strikes one as un-Pauline. It is true that Paul does use the verb in 2 Cor. 4.11, but, significantly enough, he uses it for the manifestation of the life of Jesus in the strenuous and precarious lives of his disciples. One cannot help suspecting that Ignatius uses it to express the epiphany of a god on earth, as perhaps it is used in 1 Tim. 3.16 (which I do not take to be Pauline). In short, it looks as if already, sixty years after the writing of 1 Corinthians, what was to become traditional Christology is at work on the interpretation of Paul's Letters, turning his astonishing claim that God is revealed in complete humanity into the assertion that God was revealed in Christ our God despite the conditions of humanity. But Ignatius' misunderstanding only serves to throw into relief the remarkable significance of Paul's assertion.

3

THE VINDICATION OF GOD

We began the last chapter with a quotation from Karl Barth. We begin this one with another. Barth writes of Christ, 'He can conduct the case of God against us in such a way that he takes from us our own evil case, taking our place, and compromising and burdening himself with it.'[1] Barth uses this phrase in the context of the doctrine of the atonement; but we may well take up from him the thought of God compromising himself. We have tended so far, in our exposition of the divinity manifested in the humanity, to concentrate on the aspect of revelation. But if our account is to be true to the witness of the New Testament, we must also understand the career of Jesus Christ as an act of God's self-giving. Not only is the cross the revelation of God's self-giving love, but in the whole life of Jesus we must be able to see God giving himself to man. The New Testament writers express this in different ways: thus we read that God sent or gave his Son; sometimes it is expressed by saying that by the design of God Jesus was delivered up into the hands of wicked men. The thought lies behind Paul's striking language about the weakness and foolishness of God. It is implied in John's presentation of the divine glory. Any doctrine of the incarnation that is to measure up to the scale on which the Christology of the New Testament is constructed must allow for this element.

The traditional Chalcedonian Christology certainly could allow for this; according to it, God did give himself in Christ. It is true that the extent to which he gave himself had its limits: the Word incarnate was not normally regarded as having accepted human limitations of knowledge, and certainly not the conditions of a human personality. But this Christology could certainly say that God gave himself in the incarnate Word. We have declined to follow the Christology of hypostatic union and two natures;

we are presenting a Christology of a completely human Jesus in whom God the Word was uniquely revealed. On the basis of this Christology, how far can we say that God gave himself in Christ?

We have claimed so far, following the lead of Paul, John, and Hebrews, that God is known in the complete human obedience of Christ, an obedience made perfect in suffering. This suffering obedience revealed God's nature because it was undertaken by God's will. Jesus in going to the cross was carrying out the Father's will. But, if God asked this of Jesus, God was so to speak committing himself or compromising himself in the career of his unique servant. By demanding and accepting Jesus' offering of his life God pledged himself to mankind: this great act of faith must not be in vain. If God is the sort of God who manifests himself in the suffering and death of his obedient servant, he must also vindicate the servant and thereby vindicate himself.

But another conclusion follows: rejecting the Christology of the unique God-man, we have claimed to find in Scripture a Christology of the uniquely obedient man, supreme medium of God's revelation of himself. We ought in that case to be able to trace an imperfect or approximating revelation through the same sort of medium under the old dispensation. If God was revealed at all in Israel's history (and we cannot possibly dispense with this assumption), we might expect that he would have been revealed in some sort of way approximating to the supreme revelation in Christ. We turn therefore to the Old Testament to see whether there we can find any trace of God active in the suffering obedience of his servants.

The figure of the prophet Jeremiah suggests itself at once. Here is someone who is a solid, three-dimensional figure in history, as many of Israel's traditional heroes are not; someone, moreover, who left a very remarkable record of his communion with God; someone who suffered because of his obedience to God's call. We shall proceed, therefore, to examine part of that element in the Book of Jeremiah which is often called 'the confessions of Jeremiah'. Our aim will be to see how far God may be said to have compromised himself in Jeremiah's career; how far the obedience of the prophet can be seen as a revelation of God's nature; how far Jeremiah's desire for vindication can be said to point to the need for some act of vindication on God's part. We have confined ourselves to the 'confessions' because it is here that we find the deepest expressions of Jeremiah's religious experience; and also because here we are closest to contemporary history. Much of the Book of Jeremiah, according to the experts, is history to some extent at second hand, a reconstruction during the exile of what Jeremiah must have said and done a generation earlier. In the 'confessions' we seem to be meeting Jeremiah as a contemporary.

We begin with Jer. 11.18–20, where Jeremiah protests his innocence of the plots laid against him:

> The Lord made it known to me and I knew;
> then thou didst show me their evil deeds.
> But I was like a gentle lamb led to the slaughter.
> I did not know it was against me they devised schemes . . .
> But, O Lord of hosts, who judgest righteously,
> who triest the heart and the mind,
> let me see thy vengeance upon them,
> for to thee have I committed my cause.

It seems to be Jeremiah's own kith and kin who were plotting against him. We should notice not only Jeremiah's plea for vengeance but also the fact that he commits his cause to God. In faith he looks to God for ultimate vindication.

In 12.1–6 Jeremiah's cry grows more urgent; moreover we have God's reply:

JEREMIAH
> Righteous art thou, O Lord, when I complain to thee;
> yet I would plead my cause before thee.
> Why does the way of the wicked prosper?
> Why do all who are treacherous thrive?
> Thou plantest them, and they take root;
> they grow and bring forth fruit;
> thou art near in their mouth
> and far from their heart.
> But thou, O Lord, knowest me;
> thou seest me and triest my mind towards thee.
> Pull them out like sheep for the slaughter,
> and set them apart for the day of slaughter . . .

GOD

If you have raced with men on foot, and they have wearied you,
how will you compete with horses?
And if in a safe land you fall down,
how will you do in the jungle of the Jordan?

This passage inspired that splendid but grim sonnet of Gerard Manley Hopkins, 'Thou art indeed just, Lord, if I contend'. Here was another servant of God who found that obedience entailed suffering and whose (historical) vindication came a considerable time after his death. God's answer to Jeremiah is anything but consoling. He simply says: 'Do you find this hard? It is nothing to what will follow.' Weiser well compares the Book of Job, where exactly the same complaint is made about the prosperity of the wicked.[2] Except that Job is a literary and not an historical character, we might well have used him also as one example of what we are seeking. Certainly God's reply to Jeremiah here suggests that to suffer for God is a duty; not till we come to Paul, reflecting on the significance of Jesus Christ, do we rise to the realization that it is a privilege (see Phil. 1.29).

The next passage, 15.15–21, leads us deeper into the fascinating dialogue between Jeremiah and God:

JEREMIAH

O Lord, thou knowest;
remember me and visit me,
and take vengeance for me on my persecutors.
In thy forebearance take me not away;
know that for thy sake I bear reproach.
Thy words were found, and I ate them,
and thy words became to me a joy
and the delight of my heart;
for I am called by thy name,
O Lord, God of hosts.
I did not sit in the company of merrymakers,
nor did I rejoice;
I sat alone, because thy hand was upon me,
for thou hadst filled me with indignation.
Why is my pain unceasing,
my wound incurable,

refusing to be healed?
Wilt thou be to me like a deceitful brook,
like waters that fail?

GOD
If you return, I will restore you,
and you shall stand before me.
If you utter what is precious and not what is worthless,
you shall be as my mouth . . .
And I will make you to this people
a fortified wall of bronze;
they will fight against you,
but they shall not prevail over you.

Weiser would mitigate Jeremiah's apparently vindictive plea
for vengeance by pointing out that Jeremiah is concerned for
God's honour rather than his own. The pain that Jeremiah suffers
is the result of the tension between the message of doom which he
must utter and his sympathy for his people. We find here the
the first signs of Jeremiah's really audacious accusation against
God which comes to fuller expression later on: God seems to be
deceiving him. Rudolph says the verse describing Jeremiah's joy
in God's word enhances his sense of outrage: he has always
welcomed God's word, but look at the outcome![3] The promise
made at the time of the prophet's call, 'I will be with you', is not
being fulfilled. God's answer implicitly rebukes Jeremiah for his
complaint and repeats the promise.

The next passage, 17.14–18, reproduces the themes we have
already met, with one interesting addition:

Heal me, O Lord, and I shall be healed;
save me, and I shall be saved;
for thou art my praise.
Behold, they say to me,
'Where is the word of the Lord?
Let it come!'
I have not pressed thee to send evil,
nor have I desired the day of disaster,
thou knowest;
that which came out of my lips

was before thy face.
Be not a terror to me;
thou art my refuge in the day of evil.
Let those be put to shame who persecute me,
but let me not be put to shame.

Jeremiah's opponents have accused him of being a defeatist and of desiring ruin for Judah. Evidently disaster has not yet arrived. The new element here is God's 'terrifying' Jeremiah. It seems to mean that Jeremiah is in danger of losing his faith, not in God's existence (impossible for a Hebrew of his day), but in the reality of his own call.[4] One is reminded of Gethsemane: 'My soul is very sorrowful even to death.'

The next passage, 18.18–23, need not be quoted in full. Jeremiah begins by claiming that he has received evil in return for good:

Is evil a recompense for good?
Yet they have dug a pit for my life.
Remember how I stood before thee
to speak good for them,
to turn away thy wrath from them.

Then follows an appalling curse on his adversaries: their children are to be killed; their wives are to become widows; their sin is not to be forgiven. Weiser believes that the actual details of the vengeance prayed for are influenced by liturgical traditions, if that is any mitigation (just as an Anglican has to say he is a miserable sinner at public worship, whether this expresses his own sentiments or not), Rudolph wisely remarks that we must not try to turn Jeremiah into a Christian. The contrast with Christ is sharpest at this point.

The last passage is the most important and the most daring, 20.7–18. We do not need to reproduce it all.

O Lord, thou hast deceived me,
and I was deceived
thou art stronger than I,
and thou hast prevailed.
I have become a laughingstock all the day;
every one mocks me.
For whenever I speak, I cry out,

I shout, 'Violence and destruction!'
For the word of the Lord has become for me
a reproach and derision all day long.
If I say, 'I will not mention him,
or speak any more in his name,'
there is in my heart as it were a burning fire
shut up in my bones,
and I am weary with holding it in,
and I cannot.
For I hear many whispering.
Terror is on every side!
'Denounce him! Let us denounce him!'
say all my familiar friends,
watching for my fall.
'Perhaps he will be deceived,
then we can overcome him,
and take our revenge on him.'
But the Lord is with me as a dread warrior;
therefore my persecutors will stumble,
they will not overcome me . . .
O Lord of hosts, who triest the righteous,
who seest the heart and the mind,
let me see thy vengeance upon them,
for to thee have I committed my cause.

There follows a brief hymn of thanksgiving and then in verses
14–18 comes a grim curse upon the day on which the prophet
was born. It must have some connection with Job 3, which is
so like it. It ends with the words

Why did I come forth from the womb
to see toil and sorrow,
and spend my days in shame?

The really astonishing feature in this passage is Jeremiah's open
accusation that God has deceived him. The word in Hebrew can
be used for a man seducing a girl. This is Jeremiah's version of
'My God, my God, why hast thou forsaken me?' The deception
consists in the fact that at the time of Jeremiah's call God had
promised to be with the prophet; in fact God has left him to be

the object of his enemies' mockery. Rudolph rightly emphasizes that Jeremiah's frankness is a tribute to his integrity: he can neither have the satisfaction of seeing his enemies overthrown nor the relief of abandoning his prophetic mission. Despite a total lack of belief in any life with God after death, Jeremiah never contemplates suicide. Nor does he give up his mission, for all the pain it brings him. Here is sheer obedience to God, without joy (contrast Heb. 12.2), and without forgiveness. His only hope lies in vengeance on his enemies; his only reward that his life will be spared. It is immensely impressive, but is still very far indeed from the completeness of the revelation in Jesus Christ.

As one reviews this amazingly intimate argument between Jeremiah and God, one is struck by two things, the absolute centrality of obedience, and the extraordinary concreteness of the word of God in Jeremiah's eyes. Bright rightly stresses the part that faith plays in Jeremiah's career, but faith is the necessary accompaniment of obedience.[5] And obedience involves suffering. Indeed one wonders whether suffering is not a necessary part of true obedience, and one is naturally drawn to speculations about the cross which have their proper outcome in what Paul says about human weakness in the service of God. As for Jeremiah's concept of the word of God, one cannot help connecting it with the prologue in the Fourth Gospel. Weiser describes the word in the Book of Jeremiah as 'a part of a powerfully operating event, in which the prophet sees himself involved'.[6] Jeremiah saw it very much as coming from outside. It may be that, just because the Word was so completely expressed in the life of Jesus Christ, Jesus did not see it as coming to him from outside.

How far can it be said that God gave himself in Jeremiah's career? One could certainly say that God pledged himself to Jeremiah in the sense that he promised him support and protection in his difficult and dangerous career as a prophet. This is what gives point to Jeremiah's reproaches: God, he says, has not supported him in the way that he promised. But, despite these complaints, Jeremiah did not abandon his mission; he carried on obediently right through the disaster, and the last we hear of him is his continuing in Egypt to predict misfortune for those who forcibly brought him there. His whole life cries out for vindication. Jeremiah himself had pledged his life on the faithfulness of God. The fact that his predictions of disaster were fulfilled constitutes only a partial vindication. Is God the sort of person who abandons his faithful servants to destruction, or at least to unending shame? We think of the last line of the *Te Deum*: 'in thee have I trusted; let me never be confounded'. In the sequel God showed that he did not abandon even his unfaithful people as a whole to destruction, but Jeremiah did not live to see it. However, in the process of rescuing his people God revealed a deeper answer to Jeremiah's personal question. At the same time as he came to the help of his people in Babylon, God dropped a mysterious hint about the significance of those who suffer for their obedience to God. The 'servant of the Lord' in the work of the Second Isaiah reconciles disobedient men to God by his obedience even to death. The pattern of Jeremiah's life is thus seen to have had a deeper significance than Jeremiah himself realized. But the need for vindication becomes all the more acute: if God does carry out his supreme purposes through the life of human obedience, he must manifest that it is his hand which has brought this about. He must vindicate his servant and thereby vindicate himself. Only thus will it be seen that God was at work. Consequently, in the obedience, suffering, and humiliation of his servants God compromises and pledges himself.

Jeremiah is therefore a type of Christ. The fact that he is never so described in the New Testament is perhaps one of the strongest indications that he is an authentic type; the resemblance is real, not contrived; historical, not legendary. Apart from two references to his writings (one mistaken), he only appears as a figure in Israel's history once in the New Testament, when Matthew represents the disciples as mentioning Jeremiah in the list of guesses about Jesus' identity (Matt. 16.14). The judgement of Strack–Billerbeck on this passage seems amply justified: 'In ancient Jewish literature Jeremiah never appears as the forerunner of the Messiah.'[7] There are three references to him in intertestamental literature, two of them in 2 Maccabees, where Jeremiah hides the furniture of the sanctuary at the sack of Jerusalem by the Babylonians; and where he appears in a dream to Onias in order to encourage him to smite Israel's enemies. The third reference (2 Esdras 2.17f) is dismissed by Strack–Billerbeck as a Christian addition inspired by Matt. 16.14. The total amount of evidence does not seem to support Lagrange's claim that 'this prophet had great importance in Judaism'.[8] The references in the Talmud are chiefly concerned with explaining Josiah's failure to consult Jeremiah when he discovered the book of the law in the temple; with Jeremiah's legendary activity in bringing back the lost ten tribes to the holy land just before the Babylonian captivity; and with providing him with the attributes of a respectable Jewish saint.[9] Nobody in the New Testament tries to adapt Jeremiah to the pattern of Christ or Christ to the pattern of Jeremiah. The resemblance is therefore completely authentic.

We must not leave this study of obedience to God before the time of Christ without a glance at that other figure which seems to represent this pattern, the 'servant of the Lord' of Isaiah 40—55. Many scholars have suggested that the portrait of the servant owes much to the figure of Jeremiah[10]—several phrases in the servant songs seem to be taken from his writings (cf. Isa. 49.1 with Jer. 1.5; and Isa. 53.7 with Jer. 11.19). Certainly the servant is obedient to God's will and certainly he suffers for it. We might also observe that, like Jeremiah, 'he learned obedience through what he suffered' (Heb. 5.8). This is perhaps suggested by Isa. 49.2:

> He made my mouth like a sharp sword,
> in the shadow of his hand he hid me;
> he made me a polished arrow,
> in his quiver he hid me away.

Here the thought of the training of the servant seems to be in the background. And obedience by suffering is explicit in Isa. 50.4–6:

> Morning by morning he wakens,
> he wakens my ear
> to hear as those who are taught.
> The Lord God has opened my ear,
> and I was not rebellious,
> I turned not backward.
> I gave my back to the smiters,
> and my cheeks to those who pulled out the beard.

What is more, the servant, like Jeremiah, protests at his destiny and, like Jeremiah, is assured of God's ultimate vindication (49.4):

> But I said 'I have laboured in vain,
> I have spent my strength for nothing and vanity;
> yet surely my right is with the Lord
> and my recompense with my God.'

God's answer comes in 49.8:

> In a time of favour I have answered you,
> in a day of salvation I have helped you;
> I have kept you and given you
> as a covenant to the people.

This undoubtedly implies also that the servant, like Jeremiah and Jesus, is a man of faith, since in verse 4 after his protest he expresses his faith in God's ultimate vindication.

The servant of the Lord is therefore a relevant figure for our inquiry: the essential features of Jeremiah's relation to God are repeated and reinforced in the picture of the servant which we find in Isa. 40—55. The servant acts as a link between the figure of Jeremiah and the figure of Jesus, because, though Jeremiah is not regarded by New Testament writers as a type of Christ, the servant certainly is; so that through the figure of the servant of the Lord much that is characteristic of Jeremiah passed into the tradition which Jesus inherited.

To this two objections might be made. First, it might be said that the great value of Jeremiah from our point of view is that he is a completely historical character and that his religious experience is firmly fixed in history. This cannot be said with equal confidence about the servant of the Lord. Thus it might be maintained that Jeremiah is in fact the only well-documented example of this sort of obedience which we possess in the Old Testament, and as such is of less significance. But we can reply that the actual historicity of the servant is not quite so important from our point of view. If we are willing to admit that Jeremiah's experience was, so to speak, caught and transmitted by means of the figure of the servant described in Second Isaiah, we can regard the servant songs as the vehicle by means of which the essential truth in Jeremiah's obedience was conveyed through

E

the centuries down to the time of Jesus. It is not, however, by any means universally agreed among scholars that the servant is a totally unhistorical figure. Such a view would be tantamount to maintaining that in the servant we have an ideal figure, an aspiration for ideal Israel, for some ideal remnant in the future. In fact this view seems to be rather out of favour today, and weighty support can be found for the theory that in the picture of the servant we have recorded the experience of the prophet himself, or at any rate a record of the impression he made on his closest disciples. If so, then the servant may be considered as a brilliant example of one who learned obedience through what he suffered, and just because of the connection between the servant and Jesus, the servant's example can be said strongly to reinforce the pattern of obedient suffering which we have been seeking to trace in the Old Testament.

The second objection is of a different nature. It consists in the claim that Jesus never thought of himself as the servant. This category, it has been maintained, was applied to him only relatively late in the formation of the New Testament tradition, in the work of Luke and 1 Peter. To this we would reply that such a conclusion is not justified by the evidence. In the very earliest written documents, the Pauline letters, Jesus is already identified with the servant. The fact that Paul does not in so many words describe him as *pais theou* or *doulos theou* is not by any means decisive. He assumes that Jesus came as the servant in accordance with Scripture, and sometimes specifically refers to Isa. 52.13—53.12 (see Rom. 4.25; 10.15; 15.8,21; Phil. 2.7; 2 Cor. 6.2). We are perhaps in danger of reading into the New Testament what is really a nineteenth-century category, 'the servant of the Lord of Second Isaiah'. Naturally early Christians had no conception of any such thing. They thought of the obedient, suffering servant, true representative of God's people, who could be heard speaking equally in the Psalms and the prophets. His protests and prayers could be heard by those who had ears of faith.[11] In view of this it is not rash to suggest that Jesus also saw himself as the servant in this sense. Not that he consciously identified himself with 'the servant of the Lord' of Isa. 53, but that he did see himself cast in the role of the obedient servant Israel. His references to himself as servant agree with this, and so does his conviction that he must die for Israel. Although the form in which this conviction is expressed in the Synoptic Gospels is certainly influenced by hindsight about the way in which his death took place, this does not justify us in concluding that the prophecy of his death is an invention of the early Church. The very poignant and significant quotation of Ps. 22 recorded as uttered on the cross is entirely in line with this also. Thus in the widest and most important sense we may reasonably claim that Jesus did see himself as the servant, a servant, moreover, whose essential vocation lay in being all, and more than all, that Jeremiah was.

In any case the vital question is: did Jesus exhibit the pattern of the servant? About this there can be no doubt: at Gethsemane, on the cross, we see the most essential features of the vocation equally of Jeremiah and of the servant perfectly reproduced: obedience to the will of God even to the extent of terrible suffering and death; uncertainty, protest perhaps, but ultimate faith in God's vocation and vindication—all these are more clearly represented in Jesus even than in Jeremiah. If we agree that God's self-giving is revealed in suffering human obedience, we can trace a clear and growing revelation from Jeremiah through the servant of the Lord to Jesus, in whom the revelation reaches its climax.

The question may well be asked: how is Jesus different from Jeremiah? What is unique about the way in which God gave himself, compromised himself, and pledged himself in Jesus as compared with Jeremiah or the servant of Second Isaiah? To this we give an answer that covers three points:

1. Jesus was superior in the completeness of his obedience. His protest is less violent. He accepts death with open eyes. He understands himself as destined for death by God's will. This cannot be said at all of Jeremiah, or with any sort of certainty about the servant.

2. The election of God makes Jesus different. This point is well made by both D. M. Baillie and Pittenger.[12] It was not just anyone who obeyed, who suffered, who rose again. It was Jesus Christ. We must of course say the same thing for Jeremiah: he too was elect of God, he too could not have done what he did

had he been someone else. But the election of each was different: Jeremiah was a prophet. It is probably as much owing to him as to anyone else that Israel survived the exile, that Israel's record of revelation was preserved. Jesus' election was different just because it was on a greater scale. He was called to be the servant of Israel, the Messiah, the Son, the means of God's eschatological revelation, the perfect instrument of the Word of God. Through him the God of Israel was made fully known not only to Israel but also to the Gentile world. Through him Judaism was transformed and the course of world history profoundly affected. The concreteness of God's revelation is involved here. Jesus came in the fullness of time as Jeremiah did not. Barth very interestingly links the theme of 'the fullness of time' with the theme of the servant when he writes: 'Because it is inevitable that offence should be taken at revelation, at "God in time", the form of the revelation is necessarily the Isaianic–Pauline "form of a servant", the unapparent and unknown form in which it is true that "the fulfilled time" is the time of the years 1–30.'[13]

3. Neither Jeremiah nor the servant of Second Isaiah can be said to have revealed in their lives of obedience the ḥesed, the love or mercy of God, as Jesus did. This is perhaps as important a consideration as any. We have carefully traced the way in which the writers of the New Testament regard Jesus as the revelation of God's essential attributes, mercy and faithfulness. In the careers of Jeremiah and of the servant there is little or no sign of this mercy. On the contrary, Jeremiah, as we have observed, pleads with God for vengeance on his enemies, sometimes using the most bitter and violent language. It is not for us to pass judgement on him because he was not a Christian, but the point here is that he was not a Christian. Jesus is infinitely superior, and therefore infinitely more the instrument and medium of God's revelation in that he does manifest in his life the love and forgiveness of God. The temptation is to make a neat division here, and to say that Jesus revealed both the ḥesed and the 'emeth of God, whereas Jeremiah and the servant of Second Isaiah revealed only the 'emeth. But this temptation should be resisted. We have argued in the last chapter that the relation of the Son to the Father in the Fourth Gospel (which is the obedience of

Jesus) reveals God's self-giving love. Hence we must not try to argue that we can learn nothing about God's love from the obedience of Jeremiah or of the servant. But we must hold that it is a more indirect revelation. Directly neither Jeremiah nor the servant communicated anything of God's mercy. In this respect they are infinitely different from Jesus Christ.

Nobody suggested in Jeremiah's lifetime that he represented a revelation from God. Only afterwards was it seen that God really had spoken through him. The careful preservation of his words is an indication of this. Indeed the fact that his daring dialogue with God was preserved suggests that Jewish orthodoxy did not consider it incompatible with his having been God's messenger. The Second Isaiah, when he described the figure of the servant of the Lord, did not present him in terms of a divine being or of anything like an incarnation. The servant may have been regarded by some as the Messiah, or as a picture of the Messiah. He is, however, described as having been called, trained, and designated by God. His offering of himself seems to have been thought of as acting on God in a manner remarkably reminiscent of the transactional atonement theory of classical Christian theology (see Isa. 53.4–5), and undoubtedly he formed part of God's redemptive design. Thus we can trace an approximation (but only an approximation) to what was later said of Jesus.

However, when all is said and done, the essential link between Jeremiah, the servant of Second Isaiah, and Jesus is obedience. The centre of obedience lies in the will. According to the Epistle to the Hebrews it is the will that is the kernel of Jesus' offering, and in his will that we can offer our wills (see Heb. 10.9–10). The human will is the line along which the revelation of divinity runs. It is the point at which the humanity and the divinity most specifically coincide. It is the linch-pin of the doctrine of the incarnation.

Perhaps when we give deeper consideration to Jeremiah's apparently deplorable prayers for retribution on his enemies, we may find something of greater significance in them. They were his only means of seeking vindication. But, as we have seen, vindication played an important part in the careers of both the

servant of the Lord and of Jesus. The whole concept of vindication is integrally connected with faith: only he who lives by
faith, and cannot therefore see now that God is with him, will
seek for vindication. The vindication of the servant and the
resurrection of Jesus are essential parts of God's pattern or design.
But Jeremiah, though he was most emphatically a man of faith,
did not extend his mental horizon beyond this life. His vindication consequently, from his point of view, had to consist in the
process of showing that his enemies were in the wrong. In this
respect the difference between Jeremiah and the servant of Second
Isaiah is remarkable. Obscure though it be, uncertain though the
mode by which it was to be manifested undoubtedly is, the
vindication of the servant after his death does seem to form an
element in the last of the servant songs. Vindication in fact is
an essential part of obedient suffering as a revelation of God's
self-giving, because it shows that the obedience and suffering are
God's action, God's design, God's manifestation of his nature.

Indeed we might say that the resurrection of Jesus was essential
for the theodicy. Theodicy, the demonstration in history that
God was just, is an important part of the Deuteronomic element
in the Pentateuch: both the death of Jeremiah (however it came
about) and the death of Jesus would seem to be moral outrages
in terms of the Deuteronomic theology. Either that, or the other
alternative, which is totally unacceptable, that Jeremiah and
Jesus were sinners who received their deserts. Between the time
of Jeremiah and the time of Jesus, however, a new dimension is
discovered, the possibility of life after death. This was obscurely
intimated in the record of the servant of Second Isaiah, but,
thanks to the Maccabean martyrs, became a doctrine firmly
held by an influential sector of Judaism, and certainly held by
Jesus. Thus the resurrection of Jesus is not a mere turning of the
tables, an artificial *peripateia*, an introduction of a *deus ex machina*.
It is the provision of the theodicy which the Deuteronomists
(and with them Jeremiah) demanded, but at a higher level, with
a new dimension added. The Deuteronomists were right to want
to vindicate God, even if this produced some doctored versions
of Israel's history. Jeremiah was right to demand vindication,
even though he could see it only in terms of vengeance upon
his personal enemies. And in the longest perspective God pro-

vided this vindication, but in his own terms. His own terms consisted of the resurrection of Jesus Christ, in which God vindicated his obedient servant and also vindicated himself.[14]

This may explain something which seems to be otherwise obscure or even inconsistent in Pauline Christology. Paul undoubtedly thought of Jesus as a pre-existent divine being who took on the form of man for us. (This is a problem we must look at more closely in the next chapter.) But Paul also insists that God exalted Jesus through the resurrection, gave him a name that is above every name, will put all things under his feet, etc. It is not sufficient to claim that such elements in Paul's Christology are vestiges of the primitive adoptionism which he received as part of Christian tradition when he was converted. Paul not only received these elements, he incorporated them into his own Christology. In any case the same theme is found in places where there is no question of earlier formulas being adapted by Paul, such as Rom. 14.9–12. It is also a marked feature of the Epistle to the Ephesians, which is at least by a member of Paul's school. We have maintained that in the crucifixion of Jesus Christ the essential nature of God as self-giving love is revealed. Must we not also claim that the vindication in the resurrection is essential? It is true indeed that for Paul the career of Jesus is the supreme example of justification by faith; but if so faith must be justified, and the resurrection and exaltation constitute the justification. True, the very godhead is revealed in the humiliation; but it must be followed by vindication, otherwise the victory of self-giving love will not be manifested. The Alexandrian theologians had to say that in the resurrection and exaltation of Christ it was the flesh, the human nature, that was exalted. The divine nature had no need of exaltation.[15] So correspondingly we must say that the human Jesus had to be raised from the dead if he was to be the complete instrument of the Word. Since Paul probably did not operate with a two-natures Christology, we may perhaps conjecture that he would have agreed.

Another question occurs at this point. Just as the human obedience of the Son to the Father reveals the self-giving nature of God, so the vindication and exaltation of Jesus Christ ought also to have some correlation in the nature of God. If Jesus is the human image of God, then the vindication of Jesus ought to reveal some quality in God, besides being as an action the vindication of God; just as the redemptive work of God in Christ as a whole reveals something about God's nature as well as effecting our redemption. This quality is surely God's design or *economy*, as the Epistle to the Ephesians describes it. Indeed it is no coincidence that the Epistle which puts most emphasis on the exaltation of Christ also connects the exaltation integrally with God's design. Thus in the first chapter of Ephesians we begin with a far-ranging exposition of God's design which he purposed in Christ; verse 5 runs:

> He destined us in love to be his sons through Jesus Christ, according to the purpose of his will.

The word translated 'purpose' is *eudokia*, which means literally 'good pleasure'. The same word occurs in verse 9. We quote verses 9 and 10 also:

> For he has made known to us in all wisdom and insight the mystery of his will, according to his purpose which he set forth in Christ, as a plan for the fulness of time, to unite all things in him.

The word 'purpose' here again translates *eudokia*, and in verse 10 occurs that word *oikonomia* (translated 'plan') which indicates the whole design of God in Christ. It is interesting to notice that the word *eudokia* was the one used by the Antiochene theologians to describe the relationship of the Word to the man Jesus Christ. The theme of exaltation recurs very prominently a little later in the Epistle, notably in 1.20–3 and 2.5–7.

Thus once again we find that the human will reflects the divine will. Jeremiah, the servant of Second Isaiah, and Jesus all require vindication in order to show that in their obedience they have been manifesting the revelation of God, to show that in their obedience it was God who was pledging himself. But the vindication itself brings us back to the divine will, because by the vindication we see the design of God revealed. This is how God works; this is what his nature is; this is the triumph of self-giving love. Only when suffering obedience is vindicated can we see the design of God, and when we understand the design we know him as a God of self-giving love.

This self-giving of God through the obedience of his servants is not strictly speaking the *kenōsis* of the Word of God. The word *kenōsis* has been generally used to indicate a limitation or partial self-emptying of God in order to achieve an incarnation conceived on hypostatic lines. But the approach to the incarnation which we have been outlining here would represent the manifestation of God in perfectly obedient humanity as being anything but a limitation of the divinity. On the contrary, if our exposition of such passages as Phil. 2.6–11 is right, divinity consists supremely and essentially in self-giving and hence the incarnation is, as some theologians of the Liberal school have suggested, not a *kenōsis* but a *plērōsis*.[16] Indeed the particular historical events which form the kernel of Christianity constitute according to Paul the unique way in which God could disclose his 'weakness' and 'foolishness', that is his essential nature of self-giving love. The disclosure had to be in perfect humanity and supremely in a wholly human event, the cross. We agree of course with Pannenberg that it needed a superhuman event, the resurrection of Jesus Christ, in order to identify it and complete it. But even the resurrection was not an apodeictic sign such as the Jews yearned for. It too seems to have required faith in order that it should be apprehended (Acts 10.40–1; 17.32).

The study of the self-giving of God recorded in the Scriptures has thus led us to the concept of the vindication of God, which is in fact the resurrection of Jesus Christ. But this in its turn brings up the question of the recognition of God, and to that we must now turn.

4

RECOGNIZING GOD
IN CHRIST

Throughout this chapter we shall in effect be concerned with the problems which must be faced when one attempts to relate the period of the incarnation, that is the life, death, and resurrection of Jesus Christ, to the being of God. Because the question of recognizing God in Christ is the most central of these problems for the doctrine of the incarnation which we have been putting forward, we have made it the title of the chapter. And it will be found that the problem of pre-existence, with which we begin, is integrally connected with the question of recognizing God. Both the question of the Trinity in section 3 of this chapter and the four problems which we discuss in the last section, though most of them have a bearing on the problem of recognition, are linked together by the fact that they arise because of the need to relate the period of the incarnation to our doctrine of God.

1

Anyone who attempts to present an adequate account of the doctrine of the incarnation must at some point face the question of pre-existence. In Paul, in Hebrews, and in John (not to mention other parts of the New Testament)[1] Christ is presented as a pre-existent divine being and is regarded as one who is continuous in existence with Jesus of Nazareth. This divine being is thought of not merely as having been the agent of creation, and as having existed with God perhaps from all eternity, certainly from before creation; but also as having appeared on various occasions in Israel's history. The problem raised by this doctrine is twofold: we find it very difficult, if not impossible, to believe in such a

pre-existent divine being, largely because the evidence that
convinced the New Testament writers of his existence does not
convince us. And secondly, such a doctrine seems to put a question mark against the approach to the incarnation which we have
been defending. Surely, if the New Testament writers believed
that a pre-existent divine being was continuous in existence with
Jesus of Nazareth, they must have held some sort of a doctrine
of a God-man, and our thesis of the divinity as manifested in
the humanity must conflict with this.

It is only relatively recently that this problem has become
acute. A scholar such as Creed, who lived only forty years ago,
could write: 'We cannot be sure that any New Testament writer
has entertained the notion of distinctions internal to the Godhead';[2] and he adds a little later: 'When the New Testament
writers speak of Jesus Christ, they do not speak of him, nor do
they think of him, as God.' Five years later D. M. Baillie wrote:
'in certain parts of the New Testament, not only in the early
Petrine speeches in Acts, but also in the Epistles we seem to find
the elements of a Christology which makes Christ a superhuman being and yet not quite a divine being: a being quite
distinct from God and yet subordinate to him.'[3] But the work of
such men as W. L. Knox in this country and A. Feuillet in France
has now made it clear that Paul held a Wisdom-Christology in
all but name not only in Colossians (which may be deutero-
Pauline), but also in Romans and 1 Corinthians, and it is very
hard to deny that this sort of Wisdom-Christology implies the
existence of a distinction within the godhead.

In this connection it has often been pointed out that New
Testament writers (with the exception, perhaps, of the author of
the Pastoral Epistles) tend to refrain from applying the word
theos (God) to Jesus Christ, and sometimes the conclusion has been
drawn (as has in fact been done by D. M. Baillie) that New
Testament Christology as a whole is subordinationist, i.e. that
New Testament writers believed Christ to have been ontologically inferior to God. We may suggest, however, that to
draw such a conclusion is to misunderstand the intentions of the
great theologians of the New Testament. The reason why Paul,
the author of Hebrews, and John do not indiscriminately describe
Jesus Christ as God is not that they have any doubts about his

divine status: Paul in Romans, in Philippians, and in Colossians; the author of Hebrews in his opening chapter; John in his prologue to his Gospel—these all make it clear that they regard Jesus Christ as having the status of God. The reason why they apply the word *theos* to him only occasionally is that if they had applied it frequently they would have been involved in inextricable confusion. In late Judaism the name of God was not used, for excellent theological (as well as devotional) reasons. The writers of the New Testament would never have dreamed of attempting to use the name of God which appears in the Old Testament at all, even if they could have reproduced it in Greek, which is indeed doubtful. Hence if Jesus Christ was to be called *theos* indiscriminately there was bound to be confusion with the proper denotation of God the Father. This is the explanation for the fact which Rahner points out with so much emphasis, that the Son in the New Testament is never described as *ho theos*.[4] Naturally not: this was the proper description for the Father. In considering therefore the doctrine of pre-existence we are not committed to the conclusion that it implies ontological subordination.[5]

Rahner himself betrays an uneasiness about subordinationism when he writes: 'The old speculation about the Logos, which ascribed to him an activity and history in creation, before Christ but Christ-like, distinct from the invisible Father, would be well worth rethinking, after being purified of its subordinationist elements.'[6] What he has in mind no doubt is the speculation about the activity of the Logos in Israel's history which we find among early Christian writers up to the time of Arius. This tendency to identify Christ as active in many incidents of Old Testament narrative received a rude check at the time of the Arian controversy, since the Arians readily accepted this tradition and used it as proof that the Son, as visible and audible agent of God, was necessarily subordinate to the invisible Father. Augustine firmly refuses to indulge in any such speculations. What Rahner seems not to have realized is that this speculation is deeply rooted in the New Testament itself.[7]

J. A. T Robinson, in his recent book *The Human Face of God*, has put forward a theory which would dispense with the problem of pre-existence altogether. He devotes a whole chapter to the attempt to show that by their doctrine of pre-existence Paul, the author of Hebrews, and John did not mean to identify 'an individual substance of a rational nature', but they meant that 'a life, power, or activity (whether divine or spiritual) which is not as such a person comes to embodiment and expression (whether partial or total) in an individual human being', i.e. the Jesus of history.[8] On a previous page (p. 148) Robinson has agreed with John Knox that 'we can have the humanity without the pre-existence and we can have the pre-existence without the humanity. There is absolutely no way of having both.' This is a challenge to an important element in New Testament Christology that cannot be ignored.

Robinson then goes on to examine in detail the Epistle to the Hebrews, the works of Paul, and the Fourth Gospel, in order to show that a personal pre-existence was not intended by any of these writers. In each case it seems to me that he has simply failed to take into consideration the evidence that in fact these three writers did believe that Christ was a pre-existent distinct divine being. It is surely very unlikely indeed that the two remarkable words which the author of Hebrews applies to Christ in his first chapter, *apaugasma* and *kharaktēr*, should not denote a divine being of some sort (Heb. 1.3): the Book of Wisdom applies *apaugasma* to the divine Wisdom, and Philo uses both nouns of his Logos. But quite apart from this, there is evidence that the author of Hebrews did think of the pre-existent Christ as active in Israel's history, just as Paul did. I have examined the evidence in the book referred to above; it must at least be explained away before Dr Robinson's thesis can be regarded as established.[9]

Very much the same thing can be said about Dr Robinson's treatment of the evidence from Paul. If he wishes to prove his thesis with respect to Paul's writings he must explain the meaning of 1 Cor. 10.1–11 and 2 Cor. 8.9. In the first passage Paul identifies the pre-existent Christ as the source of the manna and the water in the wilderness and definitely implies that Christ accompanied the Israelites in their wanderings, probably in the form of the angel in the pillar of cloud. If this is not the conception of a distinct divine being, the burden of proving such a thesis lies with those who maintain it. Robinson does not mention this passage. Nor does he mention 2 Cor. 8.9:

> You know the grace of our Lord Jesus Christ, that though he was rich, yet for your sake he became poor, so that by his poverty you might become rich.

On the face of it, this seems very like a presentation of Jesus as a pre-existent divine being who humbled himself to our condition. One might also point to the implications of the citation of Isa. 40.13 and Job 41.11 in Rom. 11.34–5. Most commentators who have studied this passage would agree that behind it lies the idea of the pre-existent Christ as the divine counsellor mentioned in Isaiah. Robinson makes much of Phil.2.6–7, arguing that 'though he was in the form of God' does not imply pre-existence in a divine status. But we have already indicated in Chapter 2 how we interpret this passage.[10]

When he deals with the evidence of the Fourth Gospel Robinson is more ready to admit that John did have something like a doctrine of personal pre-existence. He thinks that according to John there is 'a way of having the languages both of "pre-existence" and of "humanity", if we can understand what each is doing "without separation" and "without confusion"' (p. 178). And indeed he believes that John's presentation of Jesus does attempt to do just this. Nevertheless, Robinson tries as far as possible to interpret the language of pre-existence in the Fourth Gospel in terms of eternal being with God rather than in terms of personal activity in Israel's history. Thus on p.177 he says that the origin of the Logos is 'not just the moment of Jesus' birth, but is before Abraham (8.58), before the world (17.5, 24), and indeed at the beginning of all things (1.1f)'. However, Robinson does not stay to consider 8.56, where Jesus is represented as saying:

> Your father Abraham was overjoyed to see my day; he saw it and was glad.[11]

This implies that Abraham saw the pre-existent Christ, as the Jews rightly conclude in their outraged question in the next verse:

> You are not yet fifty years old, and have you seen Abraham?

It is very difficult to avoid the conclusion that according to

John the pre-existent Christ had appeared to Abraham. If we wish to know when, I believe the answer is hinted at in 8.40, where Jesus says:

> you seek to kill me, a man who has told you the truth which I heard from God; this is not what Abraham did.

In other words, Abraham believed a man who told him the truth which he had heard from God. There can be little doubt that this man is one of the three angels referred to in Gen. 18.1–21, he whom Abraham addresses as 'My Lord' (18.3). The truth told to Abraham concerned his son; but no doubt John knew of the rabbinic tradition that Abraham was on this occasion told about the future of his race. Thus John believed that the pre-existent Christ had appeared to Abraham at the oaks of Mamre, a very personal appearance indeed. In addition to this, Robinson ignores another passage where John quite explicitly identifies the pre-existent Christ with an Old Testament theophany. This is John 12.41, where Isa. 6.10 is first cited, then John comments:

> Isaiah said this because he saw his glory and spoke of him.

That is to say, John believes that Isaiah's famous vision in the temple was a vision of the pre-existent Christ.

Thus Robinson's attempt to explain away the doctrine of personal pre-existence has not dealt with the main bulk of the evidence in favour of this doctrine. If he wishes to pursue this theme it will be necessary for him to give it more detailed attention than he has been able to do in *The Human Face of God*. In the meantime the problem remains for us to tackle.

A much more realistic approach to the question is taken by Professor John Macquarrie: he would distinguish between 'primordial being' of God (pre-existence) and 'expressive being' (Jesus Christ).[12] Pre-existence for the New Testament writers, he says, meant that the initiative lay with God. Schoonenberg has also attempted to explain away the New Testament doctrine of pre-existence, but with no better success than Robinson.[13]

We begin, as J. A. T. Robinson does, with the evidence of Hebrews, because here the juxtaposition of pre-existence and personal humanity is clearer than anywhere else in the New Testament. We have already argued that the author of Hebrews believed both in the pre-existent being Jesus Christ, who was the reflection and stamp of God's nature, and in the fully human person Jesus Christ; and we drew the conclusion that for the author of Hebrews full personal humanity must itself constitute the reflection and stamp of God's nature (see Chapter 2). The pre-existent divine being has thus manifested himself in the mode of Son (see Heb. 1.2),[14] the completely human obedient person. In fact John Knox's antinomy is boldly accepted by the author of Hebrews: he believed that Christ is a pre-existent divine being who appeared as a real man. We must leave the antinomy to stand for the moment. But we may observe that the author of Hebrews does give us a hint as to wherein in his scheme of things the unity or continuity consists between the pre-existent being and the man. It lies in the will; Heb. 10.5–10 makes this clear.

We can now consider Paul's doctrine, where the evidence is much less clear. We can confidently assert that Paul, like the author of Hebrews and John, believed in a pre-existent divine being who appeared in Israel's history. The difficult question is this: did Paul think of the historical Jesus as *a* man? There are so few references in Paul's writings to the historical Jesus that it is by no means easy to come to a conclusion. But it seems to me that on the whole we should be justified in saying that Paul thought of the historical Jesus as *a* man, in the same way that the author of Hebrews did, for the following reasons:

1. The analogy of Hebrews is relevant here. At whatever date we think Hebrews was written,[15] the author is facing the same sort of situation that Paul is facing, and using the same sort of tools. If the author of Hebrews can hold together a doctrine of a pre-existent being and a real man, it is probable that Paul may have done so too. Moreover, in 2 Cor. 4.4 Paul describes Christ as the image (*eikōn*) of God. This word conveys exactly the same meaning as do *apaugasma* and *kharaktēr* in Heb. 1.3. It suggests that in this respect Paul had exactly the same doctrine as Hebrews has: the pre-existent divine being, perfect image of the Father (probably from all eternity) has appeared as a completely human personality.

2. Paul believed that the historical Jesus as the Messiah lived by

faith. For the evidence in favour of this assertion I fear I must refer the reader to another work of mine.[16] The evidence consists mainly in an examination of Paul's use of Scripture. For example, I take the two scriptural citations in 2 Cor. 4.13 and 6.2 as referring primarily to Christ. If this is so, there can be no doubt that Paul regarded him as having lived by faith. Indeed I believe that according to Paul Christ was justified by faith, and in this lies the ground of our being justified by faith in him. A careful analysis of the very complicated citation of Job 41.11 in Rom. 11.35 leads to the same conclusion: the counsellor (*sumboulos*) to whom Isaiah refers in the citation in 11.34 is the sole person who has successfully established a claim on God: God accepts his claim and thereby justifies him. But if the historical Jesus lived by faith, gone is the omniscience of the God-man. Jesus was *a* man, like us in all respects except sin.

3. In 2 Cor. 10.1 Paul writes:

> I, Paul, myself entreat you, by the meekness (*praütēs*) and gentleness (*epieikeia*) of Christ.

These two words denote human qualities. No one in the Old Testament attributes meekness and gentleness to God. The nearest we get is Wisd. 12.18:

> Thou who art sovereign in strength
> dost judge with mildness (*epieikeia*).

Compare also the Psalms of Solomon 5.12:

> And thou shalt hearken, for who is kind (*khrēstos*) and mild (*epieikēs*) but thou?[17]

But Paul is appealing to the mildness of Christ manifested in his historical life which culminated in the cross ('the weakness of God' is very prominent in 2 Cor., as we have noted). He does not think of Christ as a mild judge but as a mild and gentle victim. It is true of course that the meekness and gentleness of the human Jesus have great significance as a revelation of God's nature. But the revelation is in humanity; and this passing reference thrown out by Paul in the heat of controversy seems to

me to be an indication that he regarded the historical Jesus as a
human person.

4. We can even find a parallel to Hebrews' use of Jesus' will as
the connecting link between the pre-existent being and the
historical man. It occurs in Paul's use of the word obedience
(*hupakoē*). In Rom. 5.19 he writes:

> For as by one man's disobedience many were made sinners,
> so by one man's obedience (*hupakoē*) many will be made
> righteous.

We find the same emphasis in Phil. 2.8:

> And being found in human form he humbled himself and
> became obedient (*hupaköos*) unto death, even death on a cross.

The essence of obedience lies in the will. And we may well
observe in Rom. 5.19 that the parallel with Adam would seem to
suggest that Jesus also was regarded by Paul as *a* man during the
days of his flesh.

The antinomy therefore is present, I believe, in Paul as in
Hebrews. It does not seem that either author ever had occasion
to attempt to resolve it. Perhaps the first to make this attempt
was John.

We have already in this chapter given reasons for believing
that John did hold a doctrine of personal pre-existence. The
question is: did John follow Paul (probably) and Hebrews
(certainly) in holding that Jesus was *a* man with a full human
personality? On the whole it seems unlikely. The Jesus of the
Fourth Gospel is much more like a God-man. It is no coincidence
that God-man Christology invariably appeals to the Fourth
Gospel for confirmation. This is not to suggest that John held a
Docetic Christology. We have already shown in Chapter 2
how essential for John was the real humanity as a medium of
revelation. Nevertheless, it does look as if John is describing the
Logos as directly present in human form. The Jesus of the Fourth
Gospel is aware of his ontological relationship with the Father.
He remembers events which occurred in his pre-existent state.
He seems to be in possession of knowledge acquired when he

was in that state. Above all, he does not seem to live by faith: he gives the impression of omniscience.

The only strong evidence on the other side lies in the very remarkable displays of emotion which John on three occasions attributes to Jesus; see 11.33–8; 12.27–32; 13.21–30. Here language is used about Jesus which is quite as strong as, if not stronger than, the description of Jesus' emotion at Gethsemane which we find in the Synoptic Gospels and in Heb. 5.7–9. This is very strange and unexpected and constitutes one of those many occasions on which John surprises us by suddenly showing a most un-Johannine characteristic. In Greek thought emotion was the great index of humanity as contrasted with divinity. Does this not suggest that John may after all have held the same view about the historical Jesus as did the author of Hebrews? The solution, I believe, is to be found in a feature which is common to all three passages which we have mentioned, the presence, explicit or implicit, of Satan the great enemy. There are explicit references to him in chapters 12 and 13 and it is not difficult to detect his presence in the narrative of the raising of Lazarus in chapter 11. We must remember that the emotion in question appears to be primarily anger: Jesus is angry because he sees behind death the figure of Satan, who uses death as his agent. Incidentally this is a feature which has probably got much historical truth, because Jesus probably did see his ministry as a campaign against Satan. But anger against Satan is an emotion which for Jews is entirely appropriate to God. So Jesus' displays of emotion in the Fourth Gospel, surprising though they are, probably do not point away from the presentation of Jesus as the God-man.

Thus it looks as if John alone among New Testament writers attempted a solution of the antinomy between pre-existence and real manhood. That he attempted it is a measure of his greatness. The Church and traditional Christology took their cue from John and proceeded to work out the Chalcedonian Christology of two natures. One can hardly blame them, for it was the only *solution* offered in the New Testament. This is not to say that John consciously held a two-natures Christology, but he seemed to provide the materials for it. Certainly the Chalcedonian Christology would appear to follow from the presentation of

Jesus as the God-man; and it does seem likely that this is the Christology which John wishes us to accept. Perhaps the author of the First Gospel also was moving in this direction: his tendency to avoid representing Jesus as ignorant of anything; his toning down the abruptness or rudeness which in Mark's Gospel the disciples sometimes show towards Jesus; his insistence that Jesus could have saved himself by calling on God for superhuman aid—all these features suggest that he held something like a God-man Christology. But he says little or nothing about pre-existence, and he is perhaps too much of a Jew to be attracted by anything like a Logos doctrine.

The only alternative solution is to conclude that John viewed the historical Jesus as a full human personality, but one who had exceptional, abnormal, or even on occasion superhuman powers. This would mean that according to John Jesus came to a knowledge of his divinity and to a recollection of his pre-existent state by a natural process of growth. If so, John held much the same view as can be found among certain British Liberal theologians of a past generation who accepted the Liberal rejection of Chalcedon but not the dismissal of the Fourth Gospel as a source of historical information about Jesus.[18] But it must be admitted that there there is little evidence for this. These theologians came to this sort of conclusion because they were trying to reconcile Johannine Christology with Liberal presuppositions, not because they were devoted disciples of John.

The antinomy, we may hope, has been made out for Paul and Hebrews. Since we do not accept John's solution, how do we resolve it? The answer lies in a consideration of the function of the pre-existence doctrine in the New Testament. Why did certain New Testament writers (or their predecessors in the period of oral transmission for all we know) frame a doctrine of pre-existence in the first place? Since we do not accept the literalist view that Jesus told his disciples about his pre-existence when he was with them in the flesh, we must conclude that the pre-existence doctrine was produced by the early Church. Why were early Christians constrained to do this? Various answers have been suggested by scholars. One is that the early disciples were driven to speculate, not only about what Jesus did for our salvation (functional Christology), but also about where he came

from, about what his real origin was (ontological Christology).[19]
Others have suggested that there already existed a tradition of
Wisdom speculation into which the figure of Jesus could be
easily fitted.[20] I do not deny that there is some truth in both
these suggestions, especially the latter; but a still more significant
reason for the appearance of the doctrine of pre-existence may
be found when we think of Jesus, as the New Testament writers
undoubtedly did, in terms of the revelation of God. For the
early Christians, God had revealed himself supremely in Jesus
Christ. But God does not change, therefore God must always
have been as he is now known in Jesus Christ. As Jews, they
believed that God had really revealed himself to Israel of old,
in very varied ways as we are reminded in Heb. 1.1, but nevertheless no early Christian could doubt that there was a revelation
of God to Israel recorded in the Scriptures. It must follow that
the God who revealed himself to Israel of old revealed himself
then in some sense as the same God who is known in Jesus. In
other words, once grant any revelation of God in pre-Christian
times, then for early Christians it must be a revelation of God
in Christ.

We are apt perhaps to forget that the early Christians were
just as much bound to come to terms with the Old Testament as
Christians are today. In fact the question was more urgent for
them, because they had no New Testament to act as a criterion
of faith. Our solution of this particular problem was invented
in the nineteenth century: it takes the form of a theory of more
or less progressive revelation. God, we say, was only dimly
known in earliest times in Israel. Thanks to the work of the
great prophets and many others also, that knowledge was
broadened and deepened, and culminated in the revelation in
Christ. Such a theory was quite impossible for early Christians,
or indeed for anyone before the Enlightenment. Instead the
early Christians evolved the doctrine of the pre-existence of
Christ. This doctrine did for them what the theory of progressive
revelation does for us, it enabled them to claim the Hebrew
Scriptures for their own without being dominated by them.
From the point of view of their own time, they were entirely
justified in evolving a doctrine of pre-existence. The fact that
we today cannot accept the idea of a pre-existent Christ active

in Israel's history should not obscure the truth that the early Christians were quite right in their claim that God, in so far as he has revealed himself at all, has revealed himself as God known in Jesus Christ.[21]

So we may perhaps retain the intention that lies behind the pre-existence doctrine, even if we cannot accept it in detail. It is in fact a declaration of God's *'emeth*, his faithfulness. God as manifest in the wholly human life of Jesus is the same God who has always sought to communicate himself to men. This means that we must certainly recognize distinctions within the godhead, a point to which we must revert later. But we can avoid John Knox's antinomy if we decline to accept the form in which the New Testament writers expressed their doctrine of pre-existence. To claim that a distinct divine being (perhaps called Christ) appeared on various occasions in the history of Israel is mythology. To add to this the belief that the same divine being appeared as a real personal man in Jesus of Nazareth is to add an impossible antinomy. But we need not follow the New Testament writers here, as long as we preserve their intention. God in his self-communication to his creatures (which mode of being we call the Word or Logos) has always manifested himself as self-giving love, full of grace and truth. In the life of perfect obedience of Jesus Christ this self-revelation reached its climax. In him the Word perfectly expressed himself, a self-expression which was only possible through the medium of complete, perfect humanity. Thus the sonship of Jesus reveals, not directly his consubstantiality with the Father, but the self-giving nature of God. The doctrine of pre-existence as expressed in the New Testament points to a truth which we must accept. The way in which that truth was expressed through the doctrine of pre-existence met the needs of early Christianity, even though we would express it in different terms today.

2

Because we have rejected an hypostatic account of the mode of the incarnation, we have been proceeding so far on the assumption that the historical Jesus was a completely human personality, that there was nothing superhuman about him. This approach

we have shown to be quite compatible with the three aspects
of the incarnation which we have tried to expound in Chapters
1, 2, and 3 respectively, that is to say, Jesus Christ as the
personal revelation in history of God as mercy and faithfulness;
the concept of the cross as the manifestation of the divinity by
means of the humanity; and the self-giving love of God as
shown in the suffering obedience of his servants. With the all-
important exception of the resurrection of Jesus Christ, which
we have claimed was an essential act of divine vindication, this
has been an exposition of the incarnation which has not at any
point relied on miracle, on anything superhuman, for its evidence.
This does not exclude the possibility of miracle in the historical
career of Jesus, but it does remove miracle as such from the
centre of the argument. God, we have claimed, was supremely
revealed in the completely human.

But we cannot leave it at that. Behind the revelation of God
in the human life of Christ must lie some knowledge of God from
some other source. If we ask men to see in Jesus Christ the
supreme revelation of God's nature, as the New Testament
does, what we are doing in effect is to ask them to *recognize*
God in the human life of Jesus Christ. God is not directly apprehended in the historical Jesus, in the same way (for example)
that Arjuna directly apprehends Krishna as god when Krishna
throws aside his human disguise in section XI of the *Bhagavad
Gītā*. God is recognized in Christ: faith recognizes God in the
human face of Jesus. But you cannot recognize someone unless
you have seen them before, or at least seen a picture of them, or
heard a description of them, or learned something about them.
Hence those who recognize God in Christ can do so only on the
basis of some previous knowledge of God.

The traditional Christology did not encounter this difficulty
to the same extent, because it tended to suggest that the original
disciples, and therefore all subsequent disciples who accepted
their testimony, could recognize the historical Jesus as God
directly. When challenged to say why they believed that Jesus
Christ was God, traditional theologians tended to point first
to his miracles, beginning at the virgin birth; and then to assert
that Jesus himself had claimed to be God. A certain element of
recognition could not be avoided because the God whom

Jesus (it was asserted) claimed to be was the God revealed to Israel of old, and not any other God. Nevertheless, traditional Christianity did on the whole maintain that the historical Jesus could have been, and to some extent was, directly apprehended as God.[22] Our approach makes no such claim. If therefore we wish to persuade anyone that in Jesus Christ God has supremely revealed, pledged, and given himself, we must assume some prior knowledge of God.

We have, however, already indicated quite clearly the source from which this prior knowledge of God must come; it must come from the revelation of God to Israel of old, recorded in the Old Testament. Our treatment of Jesus as the revelation of God's mercy and faithfulness directly implies this: we recognize in him the supreme manifestation of God's *ḥesed* and *'emeth* because we already know God as 'abounding in steadfast love and faithfulness' from the Old Testament revelation. This is of course the way in which the first disciples and those who wrote the New Testament recognized God in Christ. The very fact that in our exposition of this theme in the New Testament we have so often referred to the use made of the Scriptures of the Old Testament by New Testament writers is sufficient proof of that. We are not concerned here with the question of whether that knowledge of God gained from the Old Testament revelation is itself based on purely human phenomena. This might be simply a question of terms. The revelation in the Old Testament is so very heterogeneous, so much a matter of 'in many and various ways' (Heb. 1.1), that it could be rash to conclude that there is any clear line to be drawn between human and superhuman. What is certain is that as far as the Old Testament revelation is concerned we cannot possibly do without the witness of religious experience. However God was revealed in Israel's history, the faith of Israel is an essential element in our apprehension of the revelation of God in pre-Christian times.

It is no doubt possible to appeal to other sources of knowledge in order to be able to recognize God in Christ. Paul Tillich would have us know God as the ultimate ground of being. Pannenberg suggests that 'the question of God', or the vague sense that there is a problem here which is often all that is left to modern man, might suffice for this purpose.[23] I would not be disposed to deny that the experience of God encountered in non-Christian religions would serve. Indeed anyone who preaches to non-Christians must start from the assumption that they already know something of God. Certainly the Muslim experience of God could be the basis for recognizing God in Christ; possibly the apprehension of God gained in the *bhakti* tradition of Hinduism might also prove adequate. But anyone who comes to recognize God in Christ by such means must then be introduced to the Old Testament. The notion that the Hindu Scriptures, for example, can take the place for Indian Christians of the Old Testament is a fond dream. For the Christian the Old Testament must be the normative, regular way by which we recognize God in Christ. We cannot do without it, though our very apprehension of God in Christ enables us in some degree to pass judgement on it.

Our approach to the doctrine of the incarnation has meant that we have made much use of the language of revelation. Such language perhaps needs defence in the present theological climate. It has both advantages and dangers. One obvious advantage is well emphasized by Pannenberg: it can help us to make sense of the eschatological element in the teaching of Jesus. The fact that the imminence of the kingdom was such an important element in the teaching of Jesus cannot fail to be a source of embarrassment to Christian theologians. No matter how far we are willing to go with C. H. Dodd's theory of realized eschatology, an honest appraisal of the Synoptic Gospels leaves one with the impression that Jesus expected the end of all things at least within the lifetime of his contemporaries. This did not happen. Was Jesus therefore completely mistaken in this vital part of his message? Pannenberg points out that an essential ingredient in Jewish eschatological expectation was that in the last days God would fully reveal himself.[24] This expectation, we can confidently claim, was fulfilled in Jesus Christ, and in this important respect Jesus was not mistaken in his eschatological expectations. This consideration also means that we cannot exclude the concept of revelation from our Christology. We cannot be content with a purely functional or soteriological account of Jesus. Indeed the fact that the earliest Christian theologian, St Paul, was not content with a functional Christology, but also produced an ontological account of Christ, should teach us that we too must attempt to relate the being of Jesus Christ to our doctrine of God. It is satisfactory that an outstanding element in the teaching of Jesus himself should show us the impossibility of avoiding the language of revelation.

The difficulty connected with the concept of revelation is a philosophical one. The philosophical approach of the school of Linguistic Analysis which is dominant in this country makes it very difficult to express how God can be known and therefore of course how he can be said to reveal himself. Attempts have been made to dispense with the notion of revelation altogether in Christian theology. J. McIntyre, for instance, is obviously uneasy about the concept and would prefer to describe Jesus in terms of redemption or salvation.[25] He adds that chronologically redemption is a first-order model and revelation a second-order model. This may well be true, but revelation is no late after-thought. It is there in Paul. In both the Testaments we find language about 'knowing' God or Christ frequently employed, and such language implies a theory of revelation. We may heartily agree with McIntyre when he writes on p. 171: 'Where there is no prior knowledge or acknowledgement of God, revelational propositions have no weight.' Indeed it confirms the necessity which we have been stressing of being able to recognize God in Christ. To know God in Christ is (at the epistemological level at least) to recognize God in Christ. This is (at the epistemological level) what faith does. Such an understanding of revelation is at the very basis of the New Testament proclamation about Christ. We cannot have the recognition of God in Christ without a doctrine of revelation. The more we are convinced that God is revealed in the purely human, the more we need a doctrine of revelation to assure us that it is really God whom we know in Christ.

Pannenberg, perhaps because the school of Logical Analysis is less influential on the continent, has no hesitation in espousing a doctrine of revelation. But for him what is revealed in Jesus' filial relation to the Father is the consubstantiality of the First Person of the Trinity with the Second, not the character of God himself. He writes: 'This differentiation, which is characteristic of the relation of the historical Jesus to God, must be characteristic of the essence of God himself if Jesus as a person is God's revelation.'[26] This seems to be in some sense begging the question: first he assumes that between the historical Jesus and God there is some ontological relation, then he deduces a distinction in the godhead from that. But we cannot *see* an ontological relation between the historical Jesus and God; we can only deduce it as an implicate of revelation. The fact that the historical Jesus is distinct from God is not at all surprising or particularly revelational. He shared that with all men. The relation of Jesus to God is, according to our argument, revelational indeed, but the revelation is through the humanity not through the ontological nature of the relationship. What it reveals therefore is the self-giving love of God, not anything about distinctions within the godhead.

W. N. Pittenger, whose approach to the doctrine of the incarnation has been to a large extent the starting-point for the exposition of the doctrine which we advocate, does not seem to be very clear on this question of recognizing God in Christ. He quotes Du Bose to the effect that 'the Godhead is manifest not in the non-naturalness but in the higher and truer naturalness of the manhood'.[27] This is plainly a statement which we must applaud. But if you accept it you must be able to say how you know that this is a manifestation of the godhead; how do you recognize God in the natural, however high and true? The answer which Pittenger offers to this question itself raises a number of problems. He says that God, in the most literal sense conceivable, *is* love, and we therefore recognize God in Christ because we recognize in him the love of God. He writes on p. 147: 'God's very essence is giving—he really is love'; and on p. 197: 'Is not God, in the depths of his being, not only loving in an adjectival sense, but actual love in a substantial sense?' This seems to be using language in a dangerously imprecise manner. When we use the word 'love' in the sense intended by Pittenger, we always mean a relationship between persons. Love in the abstract is meaningless: you cannot have love without having persons who love and are loved. It is true of course that in 1 John 4.8 we read that God is love. But we also read in the same work (1 John 1.5) that God is light. Why should we take the one literally and the other meta-phorically? When we say 'God is light' we do not mean that he comes in waves. Indeed in all these apparent definitions of God which we meet in the Johannine literature probably the only one that can be safely taken literally is 'God is spirit' in John 4.24. In order to have love, there must be a person to do the loving, so when the Bible says 'God is love' it means that God manifests a loving will.[28] Here I believe we do encounter a point where ontology is very much in order. But Pittenger never suggests an ontological unity of will between God the Word and Jesus. We might well quote Karl Barth here. Love, he writes, has nothing to do with mere sentiment, opinion, or feeling. It consists in 'a definite being, relationship, and action'.[29]

The question of recognition is also acutely posed by Bishop J. A. T. Robinson's book *The Human Face of God*.[30] Robinson sees Jesus as God's representative, God for us. In fact in his account as in ours the divinity is conveyed in and through the humanity. But he makes things very difficult for himself by accepting in his last chapter the position of Dr Dorothee Sölle that, since the coming of Jesus, God is known to us only through human love, not through religious experience or through his actions in history. This makes recognition impossible, since God cannot be distinguished from man. But if we are to see the divinity revealed in the humanity, this is an act of recognition, and recognition implies some prior knowledge of God in some other mode.

Schoonenberg is aware of the impasse into which Robinson seems to have strayed. He says in effect that we cannot leave God out of the picture in our account of Christ, as Van Buren and Sölle have done.[31] But elsewhere he uses more ambiguous language. He assumes that 'we know nothing whatever of God except from what we know of the world'.[32] Is this a denial of the validity of religious experience, or just a carry-over from an original Thomism? It requires elucidation. It is very satisfactory to find the question of recognition given a proper place in Dr Oppenheimer's recent book already quoted. She writes: 'One must have some concept of God already to attach any sense to the words "God was in Christ".' Later on she points out that there is no reason to think of Christ as the man for others if you do not relate him to God.[33]

3

Both our discussion of the problem of pre-existence and our emphasis on the need of recognizing God in Christ press upon us urgently the question of the relation of our doctrine of the incarnation to the traditional doctrine of the Trinity. At first sight our refusal to deduce distinctions within the godhead from the filial relation of the historical Jesus to the Father might suggest that we have left no room for a doctrine of God as three in one. If we cannot say that the historical Son reveals his eternal relationship to the Father, what right have we to talk about the Word or Logos? I believe that the very possibility of authentic revelation in Christ itself implies distinctions within the godhead. In other words, Karl Barth's basis of revealer, revelation, and revealedness seems a more secure foundation for a doctrine of the Trinity than the assumption that the filial relation of Jesus to the Father points to a distinction within the godhead. It is true that sonship is a thoroughly biblical concept. It is prominent in Paul, in the Epistle to the Hebrews, and in John, much more prominent in fact than is the doctrine of the Logos, which is explicit only in John. On the other hand, when we ask 'what does Paul wish to express by presenting the pre-existent sonship of Christ?', we seem to find that the answer is 'the self-giving character of God'. There are only four places in the undoubtedly Pauline Epistles where Paul uses the word Son in a context which must refer to a pre-existent relationship, Rom. 8.3, 32 and Gal. 2.20; 4.4. In all four of them the context indicates that Paul, in saying that God sent, or delivered up, his Son, means to convey that God gave himself. It is therefore, we may suggest, primarily the self-giving nature of God that is revealed in the sonship of Christ, not the nature of the eternal relationship. We do not deny for a moment, of course, that Paul believed in the eternal relationship between God and Christ, but the fact that he uses other words besides Son to indicate this relationship suggests that the eternal sonship was not for him primarily significant as revealing a distinction within the godhead. Though Son is a word extensively used in the New Testament for Christ, it does not in the Old Testament indicate an eternal relationship to God. On the contrary, there it either indicates Israel or else

Israel's earthly king. And the one obvious text, freely quoted in the New Testament as a proof-text, suggests anything but an eternal relationship (Ps. 2.7):

You are my son, today I have begotten you.

When referring to the pre-existent being, Paul can use *Khristos* (e.g. 1 Cor. 10.4; Rom. 15.3); or *Iēsous Khristos* (e.g. 2 Cor. 8.9); or *Kurios* (e.g. probably Rom. 10.16 in a citation; cf. also 1 Cor. 10.9 where *kurion* must refer to the pre-existent Christ). Paul can at least imply that the pre-existent Christ is the mind (*nous*) of God (1 Cor. 2.16); and, as we have already observed, in all probability he regards him as also the divine counsellor (*sumboulos*, see Rom. 11.34).

Similarly we have noted that the author of Hebrews uses such words as *apaugasma* and *kharaktēr* of the pre-existent Christ, and seems to reserve 'Son' for the mode of incarnation and risen glory. Certainly one would not naturally conclude from a reading of Hebrews that the relationship of the historical Son to the Father revealed distinctions within the godhead. God has indeed spoken to us in the mode of Son, but what he has said is not 'I have an eternal Son', but 'I have redeemed you through this Son'. We cannot refrain from asking what is the relationship between the Father and the Son, but the answer is given us in terms of reflection of glory, stamp of God's being, perhaps even of a priest such as Melchizedek.

Even John, in whose Gospel the consubstantiality of the Son with the Father corresponds to the messianic secret in the Synoptic Gospels, does not necessarily mean us to understand that this consubstantiality is revealed through the relationship of the historical Jesus to the Father. After all, when he wishes to expound that consubstantiality in explicit theological terms, as he does in his prologue, he does not use 'Son' but 'Word'. Indeed it is very doubtful if the sonship is mentioned anywhere in the prologue.[34] It is possible that the concept of distinctions existing within the godhead was more familiar to all three New Testament writers than scholars of the last generation were inclined to admit. For the New Testament writers what was primarily revealed through Christ was what Calvin in his commentary on John 1.18 so aptly describes as 'the very heart of God', that is God's redeeming love for mankind. The distinctions within the godhead which this revelation implied they certainly accepted. But any such distinction was an implicate of revelation rather than something itself directly revealed.

We proceed therefore with a clear conscience to base our doctrine of the Trinity on the revelation of God's nature in Christ rather than on the revelation of the ontological link between the Father and the Son. In this context the approach to the doctrine of the Trinity of the Franciscan Alexander of Hales, a senior contemporary of Thomas Aquinas, might seem helpful. He began from the principle of *bonum est diffusum sui*, 'the character of goodness is to share itself', and by this accounted both for the processions in the Trinity and for the incarnation: in other words, the self-givingness of Christ reveals the inherent self-givingness of God.[35]

It must be sufficiently obvious by now that our approach to the doctrine of the incarnation requires a doctrine of God as three in one quite as much as the traditional Christology does. We must be able to say that the Word was supremely revealed in Jesus Christ. By the Word we mean God in his mode of being as communicating with his creation in general and in particular with man. Though for the purpose of this study we have concentrated chiefly on the revelational aspect of the incarnation, that does not mean that we can afford to adopt a Unitarian doctrine of God. We must accept the existence of distinctions within the godhead as firmly as any defender of the traditional Christology.

However, there are different ways of presenting the doctrine of the Trinity and different views as to the relations to each other of the Persons within the godhead. Our inclination is to follow D. M. Baillie, Pittenger, and indeed Karl Rahner in preferring Karl Barth's way of presenting the doctrine of the Trinity, with his emphasis on 'three modes of being', rather than adopting the approach of a theologian such as Leonard Hodgson, who comes perilously close to postulating three personalities or distinct centres of consciousness.[36] D. M. Baillie has very pertinently observed that Barth's phrase 'modes of being' does not necessarily imply Modalism, the theory that the distinctions within the godhead are temporary or accommodatory aspects of God. The phrase 'modes of being' is the translation of a perfectly orthodox patristic phrase *tropoi huparxeōs*, and can in fact be a defence against Sabellianism, since it means modes of God's real nature, not mere modes of revelation, which would be *tropoi apokalupseōs*.[37]

It is true that Karl Rahner does not accept Karl Barth's formula. He prefers to say 'the one God subsists in three distinct manners of subsisting'.[38] Perhaps it is the touch of existentialism in Karl Rahner's theology that makes him avoid the phrase 'modes of being'. To predicate being of God in an existentialist atmosphere is to commit oneself to certain premisses which might be a distraction in this context. No doubt 'manners of subsistence' is more cautious. But the severe criticism to which Rahner subjects the word 'Person' when used of relations internal to the Trinity proves that he is much closer to Barth than he is to a thinker such as Hodgson.

This is not a realm in which we can expect direct light from the New Testament, since in the New Testament we do not find a doctrine of the Trinity, only the materials for such a doctrine and perhaps a question posed, a problem set which can only be solved by such a doctrine. It is quite true that, if we try to work out a doctrine of the Trinity directly from the New Testament, wrongly assuming that the New Testament writers held some sort of a trinitarian theology, we shall find ourselves pulled in the direction of certain solutions of the problem rather than others. For example, the New Testament writers, for reasons which we have indicated, traced the activity in Israel's history of a pre-existent divine being. This in itself would incline one towards a doctrine of the Trinity in which we distinguish three separate personalities, rather than towards the Barthian approach. Similarly in their doctrine of God the New Testament writers began, as they had to, from God the Father. The problem was then how to relate the Son (or Word) to him, and after that how to relate the Holy Spirit to both. This would naturally lead to a doctrine of the Father as the 'fount of godhead' and of the godhead of the Son and of the Spirit as derived from his. Rahner therefore concludes that this, the Greek view of the Trinity, is nearer to the New Testament than is the Latin view, which begins from the three Persons as coequal in godhead.[39]

But we are not driven to conclude that the Greek view is necessarily the right one, as Rahner seems to think. The New Testament
writers had to begin from one God and work towards a doctrine
of distinctions within the godhead, since the doctrine of the
Trinity is not itself a revealed doctrine but an implicate of
revelation. Whether the Greek formulation of the doctrine is
the best must be decided on wider considerations.

Pannenberg has a very illuminating discussion of the doctrine
of the Trinity.[40] Having outlined both the Greek and the Latin
approaches, he prefers a third, which he bases on Hegel. In this
the essence of each of the Persons consists in his dedication to the
others, his self-giving, of which the obedience of the Son is the
supreme image and revelation. This both supports Pannenberg's
desire to deduce the consubstantiality of the Son with the Father
from the relation of the historical Jesus to God, and grounds the
self-giving of God internally within the godhead. On a later
page (p. 341) he defines personality as being essentially relatedness,
and thus personality in God means that we must be able to find
relatedness within the godhead. This is certainly attractive, since
it means that God in himself can exhibit self-giving apart from
any relation to his creation. But it has its difficulties: if the essence
of each Person is self-dedication to the other, and if personality
consists in relatedness, are we not committed to a doctrine of
three personalities within the godhead? But this, far from constituting a third approach to the doctrine of the Trinity, would
seem to bring us back to an extreme form of the Latin view. The
confusion between the ancient term *persona* and the modern
word 'person' has led to great difficulties in the doctrine of the
Trinity. The great merit of Karl Barth's phrase 'modes of being'
(or indeed of Rahner's 'manners of subsistence') is that this
confusion is avoided. We want to say that God is always personal
(though we rightly hesitate to describe him as 'a person' or
'a personality'), and therefore God the Father, God the Son, and
God the Holy Spirit are always experienced as personal. But we do
not want to talk about three personalities. That leads to Tritheism.

It is certainly true that in John 17.24 Jesus claims that the
Father has loved him before the foundation of the world; and in
Col. 1.13 Christ is described as the Son of the Father's love. There
are also references in the New Testament to Christ as 'the

G

beloved', not all of which can be confined to the historical Jesus. There is therefore undoubtedly in the New Testament the belief that love characterizes the relation between the two distinctions within the godhead which are clearly recognized within the New Testament. Does this therefore require that we accept an Augustinian doctrine of the Trinity in which the Holy Spirit is the *vinculum amoris*, the bond of love, and love is made the constituent of the internal relations between the Persons? This would seem to bring us back to a doctrine of three personalities, since only a person can love. But we are not necessarily committed to such a conclusion. The reason why some New Testament writers describe the Father as loving the Son from all eternity was that they wanted both to place God's love at the centre of the revelation of his character and to insist on the distinction within the godhead which their Christology demanded. As long as we retain these two essential points we may well regard ourselves as free to dispense with the belief that the internal relations in the Trinity must be characterized by love, on the grounds that this view leads us too close to Tritheism.[41]

It must be admitted that, if we claim that God is essentially characterized by self-giving love, we seem to be compelled either to say that he has always loved himself, or to claim that the universe is coeternal with God as the object of his love. Neither solution is altogether satisfactory. Perhaps Karl Rahner can help us here, as being a theologian who acknowledges the greatest obligation towards traditional formulas, but who is also acutely conscious of the difficulties which they can present. Writing of God he says:

> his power of subjecting himself to history is primary among his free possibilities (It is not a primal must!). And for this reason Scripture defines him as love, whose prodigal freedom is the indefinable itself. . . . The immanent self-utterance of God in his eternal fulness is the condition of the self-utterance of God outside himself, and the latter continues the former . . . the ontological possibility of creation can derive from and be based on the fact that God, the unoriginated, expresses himself in himself and for himself and so constitutes the original, divine distinction in God himself.[42]

Elsewhere he comes nearer to the *vinculum amoris* theology without actually committing himself to it:

> There is a real difference in God as he is in himself between the one and the same God in so far as he is—at once and necessarily—the unoriginate who mediates himself to himself (Father), the one who is in truth uttered for himself (Son), and the one who is received and accepted in love for himself (Spirit)—and in so far as, *as a result of this*, he is the one who can freely communicate himself.[43]

Perhaps this is as far as we can hope to get in expressing a topic for which Augustine's aphorism is supremely appropriate: 'something must be said since the only alternative is silence'.[44]

4

We end this chapter by giving some consideration to four questions all of which arise from the effort to relate our doctrine of the incarnate Christ to our doctrine of God. Only one of them (the third) is directly concerned with the problem of recognizing God in Christ. We deal with them according to their importance for our theme, taking the most important first:

(a) *The unity of wills* We have already observed that the author of Hebrews makes Jesus' will the centre of his offering and the means of our sanctification; and we traced a parallel to this in Paul's references to Christ's obedience. We have of course repudiated the concept of a unity of substance between the Word and Jesus; but we might perhaps speak of a unity of will. This is not the sudden introduction of an element of Monothelitism into an otherwise impeccably Nestorian theory. We do not suggest that in some metaphysical fashion God the Word and Jesus shared one will. But the area of will is perhaps where God and man can come closest together. We can at least say that Jesus' will perfectly mirrored and reproduced the divine will. We must speak of God in terms of will, although we must also enter the usual caveats about using any type of language about God. We are now speaking by analogy; we are aware of the danger of anthropomorphism. But surely here if anywhere a higher anthropomorphism is legitimate, indeed necessary. Within the world of space–time what do we know that is better than a good will? We must have an image of God because we cannot think without images, and so we choose the best and purest image. We are compelled to speak of God in terms of love, but the love itself is a relationship not a substance. When we say that God is love, we really mean that he is a loving will.

It is here that the late W. R. Matthews' small but thoughtful book on the doctrine of the incarnation may throw some useful light. Matthews defines the will as the core of conscious life, and defines persons as 'moving patterns of behaviour events— that is, of events which have an inner side, desires, motives, choices'. He continues: 'the moving pattern of the will of God could be also the moving pattern of the behaviour events which constitute the temporal and historical aspects of a human life . . . The pattern of the Father's will . . . is the essential reality of the temporal personality of the Son.'[45] This is not an ontological unity of wills, if such a thing is conceivable, but an identity of wills, such that the divine coincides exactly with the human and is therefore perfectly reflected by the human. This seems to be the sort of thing that Paul had in mind when he calls Christ an *eikōn* (image) of God, and what the author of Hebrews means by *apaugasma* (reflection). Dr Oppenheimer seems to be aiming at much the same meaning when she says that we are made up of concerns and purposes. This is the very stuff of our personalities; and she quoted Austin Farrer: 'We cannot touch God except by willing the will of God.' She goes on to define this concern in terms of love.[46] Thus if we place the centre of the revelation in the human life of Christ in Christ's will, we find ourselves nearest perhaps to finding an analogy to the Chalcedonian Christology. Here, if anywhere, is the *Anknüpfpunkt* of the incarnation.

(*b*) *The glorified Christ*   What happened to the risen Jesus? This is a question which all theories of the incarnation have to answer. Traditional Christology said that the Logos continued his activity as the Second Person of the Trinity: the human nature which he had assumed could not continue on its own, but remained available for the Church, whether in the Eucharist, or in heaven, or in both. Some of the Reformers ran into difficulties sometimes when they insisted that Christ's risen body was not available for the Eucharist, since it was in heaven. This implied a space–time heaven existing somewhere.

We do not accept the notion of the Logos inhabiting an impersonal human nature from which he can be conceived as detaching himself subsequently in some circumstances. Jesus, we say, was a human person in whom the Word dwelt to a unique degree. What then became of him after the resurrection? We can only speak here with the utmost tentativeness. We are always in danger of lapsing into mere mythology. But all the same we must try to speak.

Throughout the life of Christ, God the Word had, because of his perfect obedience, used him as the unique instrument of reconciliation and revelation. After the resurrection he must continue in the eternal dimension as the humanity of God, the means whereby mankind is permanently related to God. But how? We can at least perceive how important and urgent it was that Paul should elaborate the concept of being 'in Christ'. It also means that, however fully human Jesus was during his earthly life, he is now very much more than just one of the blessed in heaven. We can understand also why Paul and the author of Hebrews can represent the risen Christ as praising God in the worship of the Church (see 2 Cor. 1.20; Rom. 15.9; Heb. 2.12). We are already within the sphere of the doctrine of the Holy Spirit. The Spirit means God acting in man, but Christians claim that he acts in Jesus Christ, through Jesus Christ, and by virtue of Jesus Christ. We appreciate why John tells us in John 7.39:

> as yet the Spirit had not been given, because Jesus was not yet glorified.

We can also understand, when we face this problem, why Paul was driven to work out his extremely obscure and difficult doctrine of the Church as the body of Christ. We must remember that this doctrine had an eschatological as well as a present significance for Paul. It may well be that the eschatological significance would have seemed to him the more important. It not only relates God to us in Christ now, but also attempts to explain what that relationship will be hereafter. Since we can only speak about that hereafter in terms borrowed from this present world, we are bound to falter. We must constantly remind ourselves that we are using the language of symbol. But such language is not meaningless. It is, as Tillich insists, the only way in which we can speak about that which transcends space–time. The risen Jesus, we claim, became the medium whereby the fruits of the incarnation are made available to men. This is not an instance of a man becoming God, but of a human life in the eternal dimension becoming the unique means whereby other human lives are related to God. He is the essential link for the communion of saints. By entering into eternal life with God after death we do not cease to be human personalities. Nor did Jesus. But he exercises his representative function still (rather only now does he do so supremely) and is still the perfect organ of God the Word. This is why Paul strove so hard to relate the risen body of Christ (meaning something much more like our modern 'personality' than the physical body of Greek thought) to our risen bodies, unsatisfactorily though his final meaning on this subject comes across to us in his writings. This is why we can pray through Jesus Christ our Lord and worship God manifested as the Word or Son in Christ. We do not worship the body of Christ, and Paul never suggested that we should. In the body of Christ we can worship God manifested in human nature.

This, I believe, is what Karl Rahner means when he writes that 'Jesus, the Man, . . . is *now* and for all eternity the *permanent openness* of our finite being to the living God of infinite, eternal life.'[47] And this also seems to be what Schoonenberg means when he refers to the risen Christ thus: 'The risen body of the Lord is the expression of the person he was and became in his earthly life . . . he does not stand on view but gives himself to be known.' Later on he defines Christ's continuing human nature in effect in terms of his being given to us and for us.[48] This would seem to lead on naturally to a doctrine of Christ's presence in the Eucharist. It is no coincidence therefore that E. Schweizer can suggest that Paul elaborated his doctrine of the Church as the body of Christ as a result of his experience of the *Eucharist*.[49] Dr Oppenheimer suggests that we can understand something of the immanence of the risen and glorified Christ in Christians if we call on our experience of Christ as present in the Eucharist.[50] Here is a remarkable coincidence of opinions.

(c) *Should the historical Jesus have been worshipped?* This sounds a scholastic question, like the well-known one as to what would have happened if Peter had celebrated mass between the institution of the Eucharist and the resurrection. But most scholastic questions have some relevant concern hidden behind them, and this one is no exception. Perhaps we may begin with the question: is there any evidence that the historical Jesus was worshipped? We are aware of course of the historical circumstances: the ease with which men acquired divine honours in the Near East at that time; the fierce Jewish refusal to offer worship to anyone except God. Westerners are not always aware how easily what looks like worship, but is nothing of the sort, can be offered on what are thought to be appropriate occasions in the East. On more than one occasion in an Indian village I have had to prevent a petitioner clasping my feet in supplication. But I was not being offered worship.

The evidence of the Gospels that anyone in his lifetime attempted to worship Jesus is almost confined to Matthew.[51] Yet Matthew in his narrative of the temptation faithfully records Jesus as quoting Deut. 6.13:

> You shall worship the Lord your God
> and him only shall you serve (Matt. 4.10).

It looks as if, in using the word *proskunein* seven times to describe how people prostrated themselves before Jesus, Matthew is indulging his tendency to divinize Jesus. We should probably conclude on the evidence that the historical Jesus was not worshipped during his lifetime.

We might go further and claim that in all probability Jesus would not have accepted worship from men. Here the evidence of Mark 10.17–18 must weigh very heavily indeed. A man runs up to Jesus and says:

> 'Good Teacher, what must I do to inherit eternal life?' And Jesus said to him, 'Why do you call me good? No one is good but God alone.'

No doubt there are critics who maintain that this episode was invented by the early Church in order to restrain a tendency to ascribe sinlessness to Jesus. In view of the evidence of the rest of the New Testament (and notably Matt. 19.17), it would seem very unlikely that many early Christians would wish to restrain this tendency. At any rate I regard this logion as conveying authentic information about Jesus. If Jesus rejected the attribution of goodness to himself, is it likely he would have accepted worship, with its implications of divinity?

Thus the important question hidden behind the scholastic one is: can Jesus Christ be the unique revelation of God if he was not conscious of being God himself? I would unhesitatingly answer Yes. Indeed I would go so far as to say that, since we have agreed that Jesus is the unique revelation of God's nature which could only be made through human obedience, he would not have been the revelation of God if he had known that he was God or if he had claimed to be God. 'No one is good but God alone.' All human goodness comes from God, and God can only therefore be revealed in humanity if it is a mode of revelation that points away from itself to God. The very revelation can be made only through human self-abnegation.

This leaves our question still unanswered. In the form in which it is put, it is perhaps unanswerable. Here we must applaud the wisdom of Pannenberg when he maintains that Jesus Christ could only be known to be both God and man at and after his resurrection. No one is to be blamed for not worshipping Jesus during his earthly life. But suppose that they had done so? Suppose the story of the Magi were history and not legend? Would they have been wrong in seeking to worship the baby Jesus? Matthew does not think so; and, later on in Jesus' life, we cannot deny that according to all four evangelists the irony of the worship that was offered to Jesus in mockery consisted in the fact that he alone had a true claim on men's worship. We are not at all concerned to deny that the disciples saw some hints of his divine relationship in Jesus before the resurrection. To worship the historical Jesus, therefore, would not have been idolatry. It would, however, have required a faith and discernment that was generally possible for the disciples only after the resurrection.

(d) *The Virgin Birth.* Why, it may be asked, has this piece of biblical evidence not been used to illuminate the mode of the incarnation? Surely the story of Jesus' birth from a virgin tells us how the Word became flesh? The main objection to the story of the Virgin Birth as an account of how the Word took flesh is that, if it does provide an answer to the question, we now know that it provides the wrong answer. Until relatively recently it was believed that in procreation and conception it was the male who provided the continuing seed; the female simply provided the necessary environment for its growth. This is now known to be a mistake. Both the male and the female contribute to the new life. Consequently, if we are urged to understand the story of the Virgin Birth literally as an account of how the Word took flesh, we must conclude that Jesus was half God and half man, the male contribution having been provided by God and the female by Mary. But in fact no account of the incarnation can possibly accept such a conclusion. It is in contradiction to the entire testimony of the New Testament and Christian tradition. In any case it is by no means certain that Matthew and Luke in narrating the story of Jesus' birth from a virgin intended to tell us how Jesus is both God and man. Consequently we have felt quite free to leave the Virgin Birth out of consideration in our study of the incarnation. The question of its historicity seems therefore to have no bearing on our study.

5

THE CHALCEDONIAN
SOLUTION

We began this work by stating that we could not accept the
Chalcedonian solution to the problem of how Jesus was both
God and man; and we gave two main reasons for this. One was
connected with the Fourth Gospel. The other was based on the
apparent impossibility of reconciling Chalcedon with the belief
that in Jesus there was to be encountered a human personality.
We have now finished our sketch of the alternative account of
the doctrine of the incarnation which we propose. But it is only
appropriate to look more closely at the traditional formula and
to pay attention to some of its more recent defenders. As well
as this we consider the incarnation theology of two distinguished
modern theologians of the continent, one representing the
Catholic and one the Protestant tradition; and also show where
we differ from the two theologians whose basic position has in
fact given us the starting-point for our own exposition of the
doctrine, D. M. Baillie and W. N. Pittenger. This chapter may
therefore be described as containing a critique of other theologies
of the incarnation.

The Chalcedonian Formula maintains that there is in Christ
only one *hupostasis*. After employing the four famous adverbs
by means of which it describes the way in which the two natures
in Christ are related to each other, the Formula continues as
follows:

> the distinction of natures being in no way annulled by the
> union, but rather the characteristics of each nature being
> preserved and coming together to form one person (*prosōpon*)
> and subsistence (*hupostasis*), not as parted and separated into

two persons, but one and the same Son and Only-begotten God the Word, Lord Jesus Christ.[1]

This *hupostasis* was the *hupostasis* of the Word and not of the man Jesus. In this sense the term *hupostasis* had its Aristotelian meaning of individuality.[2] It is quite true of course that the ancients did not have our understanding of personality; but even if they had, neither of the two orthodox schools of theology, Alexandrian or Antiochene, would have wished to attribute a human personality to Jesus Christ. This does indeed seem to be the view which the Council of Ephesus of 431 attributed to Nestorius, and for which he was condemned. But it is very doubtful if he held it.[3]

Some modern theologians have expressed more sympathy towards the Antiochene school, because on the whole they showed more concern than did the Alexandrians for safeguarding the reality of Christ's humanity. But in fact they came no nearer to acknowledging a human personality in Christ than did the Alexandrians. They too agree that the person of our Lord Jesus Christ is the person of the Logos. They criticized the Alexandrians primarily because they thought that the Alexandrian emphasis on the hypostatic union between the Word and the man Jesus ran the risk of compromising the divine impassibility and immutability.[4]

But even suppose we were to accept the Chalcedonian account of two natures subsisting in one person or *hupostasis*, it is very difficult indeed to conceive how the two natures, divine and human, could have functioned. Certainly no one so far has succeeded in giving a convincing account of this. Leo in his *Tome* represents the two natures as existing 'in reciprocity', but when he tries to describe what this means he gives the impression of the two natures, if not existing, at least manifesting themselves alternately:[5] 'the one is resplendent with miracles, the other submits to insults'.[6] Nor yet are some modern apologists any more successful, when they suggest that the incarnate Word normally restricted himself to the limits of his human nature, but could on occasion draw on the resources of his divine nature, like an aeroplane using its reserve fuel-tank in an emergency.[7] It is not so much that these explanations are inconceivable as that they are incredible. If we are driven to such shifts to explain how

Jesus was both God and man, we should begin asking ourselves whether we have not got the wrong approach altogether.

According to Sellers, no orthodox writer says that the incarnate Christ acted sometimes in his godhead and sometimes in his manhood; all his actions are those of one person. On the other hand, the practice of 'dividing the sayings' was approved at least by the Antiochene school. This meant deciding which elements in the narratives of Jesus' life in the Gospels were to be attributed to which of his natures. Nestorius was accused of distributing Christ's activities between two persons; the orthodox Antiochenes distributed them between the two natures. Even Cyril of Alexandria held that some sayings apply to Christ's godhead, some to his manhood, and some occupy an intermediate position.[8] The supreme test of the adequacy of this approach is how it deals with the crucifixion of Christ. Charles Wesley in one of his lesser-known hymns has a verse which runs:

> Jehovah in thy person show,
>   Jehovah crucified;
> And then the pardoning God I know,
>   And feel the blood applied.

'Jehovah crucified' is a bold phrase, blasphemy to the Jews, nonsense to the Greeks. Does it make sense in terms of the Chalcedonians' Christology? Only by means of the device to which we have already referred, the *communicatio idiomatum*, the convention whereby what is strictly speaking only applicable to one nature can be predicated of the other, so that the devout believer, if not the careful theologian, can speak of God the Word dying on the cross; or, what is perhaps even more difficult to accommodate, God the Word wetting his nappy or having a drink with Lazarus of Bethany. We know what Charles Wesley is trying to convey by 'Jehovah crucified', but is the Chalcedonian Christology really the best way of expressing it? Is there not a strong suspicion of some verbal sleight of hand when we introduce a device like the *communicatio idiomatum*?

According to our proposed alternative way of expressing the doctrine of the incarnation, we would not say 'Jehovah crucified' nor claim that God the Word died on the cross. We cannot, according to our understanding of the incarnation, simply substitute the name of God or the Word for the name of Christ when we are speaking of the historical Jesus. But we can come as near to saying this as does the traditional Christology, without the shifts and devices and artificialities to which the traditional Christology is driven. We would claim to see in the crucifixion the supreme manifestation of the divine nature. The crucifixion is unique because it is the death of Jesus Christ and because it is followed by the resurrection. The totally human event was interpreted by the superhuman event. God is equally seen in both, but the first cannot be understood without the second.

We must now consider a series of modern defenders of the Chalcedonian Christology, beginning about a hundred years ago and running right up to the present day. Curiously enough *Lux Mundi* has very little to say about Chalcedon. Charles Gore did not put forward his kenotic theory till later, and in any case his form of kenotic Christology depended on the acceptance of the traditional Christology. R. C. Moberly believes that the earliest disciples directly apprehended Christ's divinity during his lifetime: 'the men who had been His own companions, trained and inspired by Himself . . . taught and believed without shadow of hesitation that He was very God', a statement which makes assumptions about the Fourth Gospel that most modern scholars cannot accept. He adds: 'His life and His death were penetrated by consciousness of His godhead.'[9] Illingworth, one of the contributors to *Lux Mundi*, writing only four years after its appearance, says: 'Now to construct out of the Gospels an imaginary portrait, of One who neither worked wonders nor claimed to be divine, is to invalidate their worth, for it is to tear them literally to shreds.'[10] All that these statements prove is that English theological scholarship was not yet ready to face the full blast of the critical work on the Gospels which the Germans had already inaugurated. It is, however, very significant that the claim for Jesus' consciousness of his own divinity always implicitly falls back upon the Fourth Gospel for confirmation. In the debate about Christology, the Fourth Gospel is absolutely crucial.

Forty years later J. K. Mozley, writing in *Essays Catholic and Critical*, provides an acute defence of the Chalcedonian Christology. He is far more aware of the difficulties than his predecessors were. He admits that if the (traditional) doctrine of the incarnation is true we must expect 'a psychological puzzle'. He continues: 'unless we are prepared to say that the divine is human and the human is divine, we must admit a distinction between the two in the person of Christ and discover a relationship between them which is dependent on the fact that each of the terms "divinity", "humanity" expresses a truth about the one, whole Person.' This is elucidated later when he rejects a doctrine of immanence (such as we have advocated) on the grounds that 'He Himself and not something in Him becomes everything to man'.[11] But this would seem to be sidestepping the whole point of the incarnation: it is God in man, God present in a genuine humanity who reveals and saves. Mozley, by his rejection of the conception of a full, personal humanity in Jesus Christ, seems to have arrived at a position where he has to regard the humanity as a guise, a cloak, or an adjunct of the revelation. This is not what Paul or John means by the incarnation. In the ensuing pages Mozley stresses the uniqueness of the incarnation so much that one begins to wonder whether there is any means by which we can recognize it (a tendency we shall note in Karl Barth). But in fact he does ultimately indicate what is his criterion for recognizing an incarnation, it is the presence of miracle, since, when considering the objection that the Gospels do not really consciously narrate an incarnation, he remarks: 'The extent of the difficulty will depend on the judgement formed as to the miraculous sections of the Gospel.' It looks as if Mozley is falling back on the traditional proof from miracle in order to establish the divinity of Christ.

When we turn to Karl Barth we find a defence of the Chalcedonian position presented with all the vigour, confidence, and pugnacity which one associates with this great theologian.[12] He has an interesting passage in which he says in effect that the revelation of God in the humanity of Christ does not enable us, so to speak, to isolate that humanity and make that alone the focus of revelation and therefore the object of worship. He thus condemns the 'fairest Lord Jesus' of mediaeval piety, the 'Saviour' of pietism, the inner meaning of exalted humanity in Schleiermacher's theology, the embodiment of the idea of religion in Hegel, and (we may add) the 'man for others' of Bonhoeffer. It was, says Barth, the action of God in Christ that constituted the revelation. Christians worship God in Christ. This must certainly be accepted: unless we can say that God was in Christ, we have no right to worship Christ; and when we do worship Christ rightly we worship him as the manifestation of the Word in flesh. But the question arises: how do we know that the Word was manifested in the flesh? What are the signs of the divinity in the humanity?

A little later on in the same volume Barth writes:

> the New Testament statements about the unity of the Son with the Father, i.e. about the divinity of Christ, cannot possibly be interpreted on the assumption that the original outlook and declaration of the New Testament witnesses concerned a human being, who subsequently was either exalted as such to divinity, or appeared among us as the personification and symbol of a divine being,[13]

and he goes on to object strongly to Dibelius' formulation of the problem: 'how knowledge about the historical figure of Jesus came to be transformed so swiftly into faith in the heavenly Son of God'. Now we can well sympathize with this protest in so far as it objects to the assumption that there were no intimations of divinity in Jesus' life before the resurrection. The disciples could not so soon have come to so exalted a view of him after the resurrection had they not recognized something divine in him during his historical existence. But Karl Barth here on his part assumes that being a human personality is incompatible with being a revelation of God. After all, however we interpret the historical records of Jesus' life, we can hardly doubt that those who first encountered Jesus believed him to be a human personality: this is certainly the impression we gain from all four Gospels. On Barth's premises, therefore, the disciples at some point must have revised their original impression and come to the conclusion that this was not a human personality but a divine being in human appearance. I do not see that the evidence suggests any such conclusion. There does not seem to be any reason why we should not imagine that the disciples went on believing that Jesus was a human personality right up to the moment of his death, but that they felt themselves increasingly compelled to interpret his life in terms of God's design and purpose, so that when the resurrection occurred they had to describe Jesus as God's last word, the image and unique revelation of God. There are indeed traces of Adoptionism in the New Testament, so that the view which Barth rejects ('a human being, who subsequently was . . . exalted to divinity') was held by some early Christians, though we need not follow John Knox and P. Schoonenberg in the assumption that this was the one and only primitive Christology.[14] As for the other view rejected by Barth, that Jesus 'appeared among us as the personification and symbol of a divine being', this also begs the question in a subtle way. What is 'a personification of a divine being'? Why cannot we say that Jesus came as the revelation of God? God does not need to be 'personified' as if he were a principle or an idea. Barth has ingeniously swung the discussion away from the real point, which is 'how did the disciples know that Jesus was divine?', in such a way that he can set up a man of straw, 'personification or symbol', and then shoot it down.

Barth holds in fact that the disciples who knew Jesus during his historical life acknowledged him directly as God. The men who knew Jesus, he says, recognized him as Lord. 'Thou art the Christ' is an analytic, not a synthetic proportion (1, p. 463). The apostles, he insists, believed that Jesus Christ was the Son of God because this was their experience. It was not a deduction from this experience (ibid., p. 475). Similarly in 1, 2, p. 17, he denies that those who witnessed to the divinity of Christ first had a conception of divinity and then identified it with Christ; and in 2, p. 21 he writes: 'we have met with God, we have heard his word—that is the original and ultimate fact'. In the face of such confident statements about the origin of the belief in Christ's divinity, we may well ask how Barth knows all this. One cannot help suspecting that Barth is treating the narratives of the Fourth Gospel as if they were straightforward history, for it is most notably in the Fourth Gospel that the historical Jesus is recognized as Lord, and only there that Jesus openly claims to be the Messiah and the eternal Son. In any case, even on Barth's assumptions we are entitled to ask: why did the disciples recognize Jesus as God? The very word 'recognize' implies some previous knowledge of God. But once we admit this we have virtually admitted that they had some concept of divinity to which they found that Jesus conformed.

The truth appears to be that Barth asserts so dogmatically that the disciples recognized the historical Jesus as God because he is unwilling to inquire how they came to that recognition. In 2, p. 172 he actually claims about the incarnation: 'It comes to us as a datum with no point of connexion with any other previous datum.' Strictly speaking there can be no such datum: it would be totally unrecognizable. Barth has in fact adopted a rhetorical mode of saying: 'do not ask awkward questions about the mode of the incarnation'.

Barth quotes with approval the dictum of a seventeenth-century scholar: *non personam sed naturam assumit*,[15] and says that the Word made his own 'this one specific possibility of human existence', i.e. being Mary's son, and he adds: 'So this man was never a reality by himself.' On p. 164 he says that *anhypostasia* does not mean impersonality. The ancients, he claims, called what we mean by personality *individualitas*, and this they freely admitted Christ had. But it was the personality of the Word, not of any man. He sums it up at 2, p. 348 when he writes: 'There never was a man Jesus as such apart from the eternal reality of the Son of God.' We should note perhaps one other significant passage in Barth. At 2, p. 182 he quotes with approval a sentence from Gregory of Nyssa apropos the virgin birth and the empty tomb: 'If what was narrated of Christ was within the bounds of human nature, where is the divine element?' It is plain that, as far as the historical life of Jesus is concerned, Barth believes that the divine element is manifested in the miraculous, the superhuman.

At about the same time as Karl Barth was publishing his great work, an English scholar undertook a defence of the Chalcedonian Christology which runs on very similar lines to Barth's, but without apparently having any knowledge of Barth's work[16] Relton, following the lead of Leontius of Byzantium, proposed that the humanity of Jesus Christ should be regarded not, as in the Chalcedonian Formula, as *anhypostatos* (having no *hypostasis*), but as *enhypostatos*, that is finding its *hypostasis* in the divine Word. He claimed that human nature generally should be thought of as having its true fulfilment in the divine nature, and that therefore this solution was very appropriate to the Christian view of the relation between God and man. He argued for a single divine–human consciousness, a sort of psychological Eutychianism (see p. 208 of his work).

His thesis suffers, however, from the fact that he never faces the problem for Christology posed by the Fourth Gospel. He treats it as a straightforward, reliable source of information about the life of Jesus (p. 238). This means he can hold that Jesus claimed to be worshipped during his life on earth (p. 257), and also that he knew himself to be the Second Person of the Trinity (ibid.). Relton in fact uses the Fourth Gospel as an historical corrective to the Synoptic Gospels. He writes: 'All the questions inevitably raised by what Jesus says and does in the Synoptic records are immediately answered in the Fourth Gospel' (p. 252). This may well be a correct statement as it stands, but it cannot be used to establish the historicity of the Fourth Gospel.

For all his emphasis on *enhypostatos* rather than *anhypostatos*, Relton is compelled by his position to deny that there was in Jesus Christ a human personality. He writes on p. 193: 'We have no knowledge of an Ego which, because it was eternal, may conceivably have given Him in His incarnate state a knowledge of Himself as He existed prior to His advent in the flesh.' Having thus disposed of the suggestion of a human personality, Relton is able to refer to Christ as 'the God-man'. Quite in line with this is his assumption throughout the book that, if there was something divine in Jesus, it had to be manifested in superhuman phenomena. He writes on p. 219: 'Do not the Gospel narratives reveal him as doing things which transcend man's capacities?' And on p. 241 he says that the Gospel writers 'let us see also the Godhead flashing forth at times in miracles and in His own self-witness'. We would therefore judge Relton's defence of the Chalcedonian Christology to fail because the picture he presents of Jesus does not allow us to conceive of a human personality, and is not therefore consistent with what the evidence suggests Jesus really was.[17]

Sellers at the end of his learned work on the Council of Chalcedon undertakes something of an apologia for its Formula. We distinguish the two natures in thought only, he says, not in action. The impersonal humanity only means that Jesus' humanity had no independent existence, and he thinks to make matters more comprehensible by adopting a phrase from Pseudo-Dionysius 'a new theandric operation' to describe how the two natures appear in action.[18] This is stating the problem rather than solving it. Much the same might be said of Dr Oppenheimer's very unsatisfactory treatment of the theme. She writes: 'One must go on insisting upon God's presence in Christ in a more fundamental sense than in other human beings.' She accepts D. M. Baillie's paradox of grace, but says that it is not enough. She quotes with approval John Baker's dictum: 'When God chooses to exist within the terms of our environment a man is what he becomes' —once more a statement of the problem rather than a solution. She makes the matter doubly difficult by insisting that Jesus was 'an individual human being'.[19] As far as I can judge, the problem as set out in her terms is absolutely insoluble.

We have already indicated that our approach to the doctrine of the atonement owes much to the work of D. M. Baillie and W. N. Pittenger. If we criticize them, this is not because we are unaware of the great debt we owe to two acute and courageous theologians. D. M. Baillie begins from the premiss that, in order to be man, Jesus Christ must have been *a* man.[20] He then elaborates what he calls 'the paradox of grace': Jesus Christ was more receptive to the divine grace than any other man and therefore was both divine and human. The paradox consists in the fact that God both demands obedience of man and enables man to be obedient (pp. 116f). In God's grace manifest in the human life of Jesus we see God supremely and uniquely at work. Naturally such an approach must encounter the objection: is this not to represent Jesus as an ordinary man? Would any man who lived a life of perfect obedience thereby become God incarnate? Baillie answers that such an objection is essentially Pelagian. It suggests that the objector 'regarded the human side of the achievement as the prevenient, the conditioning, the determinative'. Only God can decide when the perfect human life is to take place, so part of the uniqueness of Jesus consisted in the divine election (p. 131). The reason why the incarnation came when it did was that only then was a man perfectly receptive to God (p. 49). Baillie denies 'a conscious continuity of life and memory between Jesus of Nazareth and the pre-existent Son' (p. 150); and on the next page he sums up his doctrine thus: 'While the life lived by Jesus was wholly human, that which was incarnate in him was of the essence of God, the very Son of the Father, very God of very God.'

Pittenger's book improved and built on Baillie's work. He begins by saying: 'No single aspect or area of our Lord's earthly life was divine; it was all human.'[21] But he adds: 'In the wholeness of that humanity God was known to be present and at work.' The unity of the Word with Jesus is moral and dynamic; he asks: 'Is there any other kind of union between God and man which does not in effect destroy the humanity or change the deity?' (p. 90). Here is a definition of his doctrine which he gives us on p. 183.

> The Word or Eternal Self-Expression of God . . . through 'the operation of the Holy Ghost' clothed himself with humanity in such a wise that a complete human life—including a human 'person' in our modern sense—was open to his action. Thereby man was given the manifestation of God in human terms in a distinctive and definite manner in *this* one life.

Pittenger does, however, go beyond Baillie in one respect: he demands that the divinity of Jesus Christ should be expressed in ontological terms. He rejects a mere moral and spiritual evaluation of Christ such as Ritschl offered (pp. 121–2). He suggests that this ontological requirement can be expressed in terms of love, and he criticizes D. M. Baillie on the grounds that he has neglected ontology (p. 197). But this ontological link, he makes it clear, is between God and man, not between God and Christ alone: 'some unbreakable ontological relationship must continue between [man] and God' (p. 239).

We have already criticized Pittenger on the score of recognition (see Chapter 4, section 2). We might very well extend the same criticism to Baillie. He never seems to make it clear what he means when he says of Jesus 'that which was incarnate in him was of the essence of God'. Since the life of Jesus was a fully human life, how do we recognize the divine element in it? I do not see that Baillie ever faces this question. But Baillie's account is unsatisfactory in another respect: he never satisfactorily tackles the problem of continuity; what, according to him, was continuous between the divine Word and the man Jesus? One could hardly complain if Baillie had made only an approximate answer to this, but he does not appear to be aware of the problem at all.

Pittenger has undoubtedly improved on Baillie's position; he has gone to great lengths to link up his account with a securely founded Logos doctrine. But his Christology is not satisfactorily rooted in the historical Jesus. He has conceded far too much to the thesis advanced by John Knox and commended by D. E. Nineham that the basis for Christology should not be the historical Jesus but the effect which Jesus created on the early Church.[22] Thus he writes on p. 55: 'The fundamental datum for the Christo-logical concern of the Church is the continuing and persistent life of the Christian fellowship.' This attempt to shift the burden of Christology from the historical Jesus to the experience of the early Church is inspired by one motive only, scepticism about the possibility of recovering sufficient detail about Jesus in order to form an adequate basis for Christology. If pursued to its logical conclusion it reduces Christianity to the role of a mystery religion. It should have no place in the establishment of a satis-factory doctrine of the incarnation.

Karl Rahner has made a most striking contribution to the debate about the nature of the incarnation.[23] He begins by taking exception to the popular idea of the incarnation: 'When our Lord (= God) walked on earth with his disciples, still humble and unrecognized . . . etc.', and he asks whether one can derive from the Chalcedonian Formula the actual human relationship which the Scriptures record Jesus to have possessed towards God. The doctrine of the incarnation, he says, does not teach that God was active among us in human form; it teaches in fact 'the true man, who can be our Mediator with respect to God in genuine human freedom' (p. 160). Such a position, how-ever, involves Rahner in considerable difficulty, since for him the Chalcedonian Formula is authoritative. He seems to be driven back on rather obscure definitions: 'only a *divine* person can possess as its own a freedom really distinct from itself in such a way that this freedom does not cease to be truly free even with regard to the divine Person possessing it, while it continues to qualify this very Person as its ontological subject' (p. 162). Is this

not saying in effect: 'All things are possible with God; an incarnation is unique and therefore cannot be analysed'? Rahner does,
however, help his position by adopting an approach quite
reminiscent of Relton, when he says that 'Christology may be
studied as self-transcending anthropology' (p. 164n.).

When Rahner views Christ from the side of his humanity he
can come astonishingly close to Schleiermacher. Thus he can
suggest that what makes man most human is his complete
openness to God. So Jesus is more completely at the disposal
of the Logos than anyone else (pp. 171–2n.). Suppose, he suggests,
that someone were to say: 'Jesus is the man whose life is one of
absolutely unique self-surrender to God.' This, says Rahner,
may very well state the truth about Christ, so long as we remember (*a*) that this self-giving presupposes a communication of
God to man; (*b*) that an absolute self-surrender means an absolute
communication; and (*c*) that this statement refers to something
not merely mental but is 'a statement about being'. On p. 184
he suggests the possibility of the existence of 'a man who, precisely by being man in the fullest sense (which we never attain),
is God's existence in the world'. Such an approach to the doctrine
of the incarnation from the Catholic tradition is a most heartening
and helpful phenomenon.[24]

Finally, we must consider W. Pannenberg's important study
of the doctrine of the incarnation, already referred to more than
once, *Jesus: God and Man*. Pannenberg begins by rejecting the
traditional doctrine: 'If divinity and humanity as two substances
are supposed to be united in the individuality of Jesus, then
either the two will be mixed to form a third or the individuality,
Jesus' concrete, living unity, will be ruptured' (p. 287). We
must approach our account of Jesus Christ 'from below' not
'from above', by which he means we must begin with the man
Jesus and not with the Logos (see pp. 34, 313). He begins, therefore, from the resurrection of Jesus Christ and works both
backward from there to Jesus' historical career and forward to
construct a Christology for the Church. The Easter event revealed
the truth about Jesus' nature. When, however, we ask 'What
was that nature revealed to have been?', we do not get a very
clear answer. He writes on p. 132 of 'a revelatory identity of
Jesus with God, which includes identity of essence'; and on

p. 156 we read: 'In Jesus, God himself has come out of his other-
ness into our world, into human form, and in such a way that
the Father–Son relation that—as we know, in retrospect—
always belonged to God's essence now acquired corporeal
form.' The phrase 'corporeal form' is ambiguous: presumably
Pannenberg means that the relation of the historical Jesus to God
was a reflection or revelation of the relation of the Logos to
God. Then 'corporeal form' is misleading, for it suggests something more material than a revelation. We have already criticized
Pannenberg's attempt to represent the relation of the historical
Jesus to the Father as a revelation of the consubstantiality of the
Father and the eternal Son.[25] But there is another danger in
Pannenberg's almost exclusive emphasis on the Father–Son
relationship as that which constitutes the divinity of Jesus Christ,
a danger of literalism. In the last analysis, to speak of the relation
of the Son to the Father is to use a metaphor, or at least an analogy.
It is a very useful one, indeed an essential one, and it appears
extensively in the New Testament. But we can imagine a point
at which as an analogy it breaks down. For example, certain
theories of the atonement press the phrase 'God sent his only
Son' so much that we are almost invited to believe that, if God
had had several Sons, the sacrifice would not have been so
painful! This is not of course to suggest that we can dispense
with the analogy, but to underline the danger of putting quite
as much weight on it as Pannenberg does.

There are other bases for Pannenberg's Christology to be found
in his work, some of them resembling what we have been putting
forward. Thus on p. 191 he writes: 'God's divinity is revealed
in Jesus of Nazareth in so far as the relationship to Jesus determines
man's ultimate destiny.' This suggests that Jesus' divinity could be
based on the claim which he made to unique authority, an
ingredient in Christology which we would be not at all inclined to challenge. Again we read on p. 335: 'This relation of
dedication to the point of self-sacrifice was the personal
community of the man Jesus with the God of his message. . . .
Only by the resurrection is Jesus' personal community with
God confirmed from God's side also.' Here is the suggestion
that the divinity is manifested in the obedient and suffering
humanity, and the presentation of the resurrection in terms

of vindication, two themes which we have included in our exposition.

Towards the end of his work Pannenberg reasserts the centrality of the Father–Son relationship for his doctrine of the incarnation, so much so that he actually goes to the length of denying that Jesus had any choice about it. He writes on p. 350: 'The thesis of a meritorious freedom of choice for Jesus' human will . . . would make his unity with God a work of his human will instead of letting that unity be something that happened to him, which he experienced as having come from God.' Thus, because he stakes all on the filial relationship, Pannenberg is compelled to give it a constitutive, ontological character which precludes that voluntary obedience of which the New Testament makes so much. His attempt to explain it in terms of religious experience does not help. He writes: 'When a mission has seized a man so unconditionally, he no longer has any choice with respect to that mission.' This is true only in a subjective sense. The Christian may say: 'I had no choice; I had to obey God.' But he does not mean that he was determined, or coerced, or conditioned; still less that he does not regard himself as responsible for his actions. His claim that he had to obey is not a plea of diminished responsibility. If the historical Son's obedience to the Father is not voluntary it has no significance for Christology.

Thus a book full of profound insights and illuminating observations proves to be a little disappointing as far as concerns the provision of a sound basis for Christology. Perhaps the truth may be that Pannenberg's scepticism about the possibility of knowing very much about the historical Jesus has compelled him to concentrate too exclusively on the Father–Son relationship. His rejection of the belief that Jesus claimed to be Messiah, Son of Man, or servant means that his Christology must be built on the narrowest of historical platforms. It also means that Jesus is dangerously divorced from his background in Judaism. At the same time we have the paradoxical situation that almost everything is made to depend on conclusions about Jesus' own self-consciousness. If one cannot accept that Jesus claimed to be Messiah, or Son of Man, or servant in any sense, is it not precarious to stake almost everything on the belief that one can establish his filial consciousness? The same type of criticism that eliminates the former claims would seem very likely to eliminate the latter. A Christology that is based almost entirely on Jesus' filial consciousness is not very securely founded.

One last word must be added. We have outlined in these pages an alternative account of the doctrine of the incarnation. It is intended to be only an alternative to Chalcedon, not a replacement. I hope we have shown that there is plenty of backing in the New Testament for this approach; but there is backing for the Chalcedonian approach also, especially in the Fourth Gospel. There will no doubt always be many Christians who will be perfectly content with the traditional account of the mode of the incarnation. Most of the objections which I have brought against the traditional account are objections which will appeal only to those who are heirs of the Enlightenment and of Western culture as it had developed during the last two hundred years. In the East, especially in Asia, questions of historicity are far less urgent, and there no doubt the Chalcedonian doctrine will never be replaced. It may be that this approach of mine, based as it is on an essentially Nestorian interpretation of the evidence, will be of value (if at all) only to the present generation of Christians in the West. I do not think this is to be regretted. Since the Church has always been able to live with a number of different accounts of the atonement, no one of which has ever been given the accolade of orthodoxy over against the others, it may well be that in this age of dissolving creeds more than one way of expressing the mode of the incarnation may be capable of being accommodated within the bounds of orthodox belief.[26] The Liberal theologians of the last century and the beginning of this one tended to glory in their unorthodoxy and to adopt an iconoclastic attitude towards traditional doctrine. Both the Barthian movement and the disintegration of theology which has followed it ought to teach us greater intellectual humility. We have presented an alternative account of the doctrine of the incarnation to the traditional one because we believed that intellectual honesty compelled us to do so, and we believe that in so doing we have not been unfaithful to the basic witness of the New Testament. But we have no desire to see the demise of the Chalcedonian tradition as long as it proves of value to Christians. We are quite content to abide by the apostolic precept:

> For by the grace given to me I bid every one among you not to think of himself more highly than he ought to think, but to think with sober judgement, each according to the measure of faith which God has assigned him.

NOTES

INTRODUCTION

1 See E. G. Selwyn, ed., *Essays Catholic and Critical* (3e., London 1931), pp. 162 and 179f, esp. p. 198.

2 See W. R. Matthews, *The Problem of Christ in the Twentieth Century* (London 1950), p. 7.

CHAPTER 1

1 The LXX renders the phrase with *polueleos kai alēthinos*, a notably feebler translation.

2 M.-E. Boismard, in *Le Prologue de Saint Jean* (Paris 1953), pp. 69f, has noted and expounded the connection between John 1.14 and Exod. 34.6. But he complicates matters unnecessarily by connecting this passage with the story of the Transfiguration, of which I can find no hint in the Fourth Gospel. He also suggests that in verses 16–18 John presents Christ as the new Moses. This seems to me quite to miss the point. Compare also L. J. Kuyper, art. 'Grace and Truth: an Old Testament description of God and its use in the Johannine Gospel' in *The Reformed Review* (September 1962), vol. 16, no. 1 (Holland, Michigan). Bultmann considers the possibility that there is a reference to Exod. 34.6 here, but dismisses it as 'unlikely' (see R. Bultmann, *Johannes Evangelium* (10 e., Göttingen 1962)). This is partly because he gives an unduly Hellenistic connotation to *alētheia* in John: it means 'authenticity, reality, revelation' (see his art. *alētheia* in *TWNT*, vol. 1 (Stuttgart 1949).

3 See L. Koehler and W. Baumgartner, *Lexicon in Veteris Testamenti Libros* (Leiden 1953) sub *ḥesedh* and *'emeth*. See also N. Glueck, *Hesed in the Bible* (new e., Cincinnati 1967); also A. R. Johnson, art. 'Hesed and Hasid in *Interpretationes ad Vetus Testamentum pertinentes Sigmundo Mowinckel Septuagenario missae*' (Oslo 1955), pp. 101–2, 108.

4 See J. Weingreen, art. 'Some Observations on English Versions of the Old Testament' in *Hermathena*, no. CXIII (Summer 1972), p. 12.

5 A. Weiser, *Das Buch der zwölf kleinen Propheten* (Göttingen 1963).

6 J. A. Bewer, *The Book of Jonah* (Edinburgh 1912).

7 W. Rudolph, *Das Buch Jonas* (Gütersloh 1971).

8 See Wisd. 15.1–3: 'kind and true' here translate *khrēstos kai alēthēs*; this illustrates the author's fondness for paraphrasing rather than directly quoting the Scriptures. Several editors note the allusion to Exod. 34.6. For Qumran references see 1QS 1.8; 4.4; 1QM 14.4; 1QH frag. 7.7 for *ḥesed* as a divine attribute; and 1QS 9.17–18; 1QH 1.27; 2.10; 5.9 for *'emeth* applied to the true teaching revealed by God or to the community as the abode of truth. The two words occur together in 1QH 16.16 applied to God.

9 For these rabbinic references see the *Babylonian Talmud*, ed. I. Epstein (London 1935 +). *Tractate Megillah* 15b, ed. M. Simon (London 1938), p. 91; also *Tractate 'Erubin* 22a, ed. W. Slotki (London 1938), p. 152; *Tractate Rosh Hashanah* 17b, ed. M. Simon (London 1938), p. 68.

10 See J. W. Etheridge, *The Targum of Onkelos and Jonathan ben Uzziel* (new e., New York 1968) in loc.

11 I have explained my position on this subject at greater length in the last chapter of *Studies in Paul's Technique and Theology* (London 1974).

12 I have consulted six other modern English versions offhand, RV, Moffatt, Phillips, NEB, TEV, and Barclay. Five of them convey exactly the same meaning as the RSV, to wit that the choice of Jacob was due to the mercy of God, not that God chose Jacob because he is a God of mercy. The RV translates so literally that the reader is left to make his own interpretation—not by any means always the worst way of rendering Scripture.

13 Boismard has noted the parallel here with John 1.14–17 (op. cit., p. 78), and Bultmann agrees that here *alētheia* means God's reliability (art. cit.).

14 R. Bultmann, *The History of the Synoptic Tradition* (ET, Oxford 1968, of German e. of 1931), p. 16. Compare also G. Bornkamm, ed., *Tradition and Interpretation in Matthew* (ET, London 1963, of German e. of 1960), p. 82; and B. Rigaux, *Témoinage de L'Évangile de Matthieu* (Brussels 1967), pp. 69–70.

15 C. G. Montefiore, *The Synoptic Gospels* (London 1909) in loc.

16 E. Lohmeyer, *Das Evangelium des Matthäus* (Göttingen 1962, rev. W. Smauch); cf. also J. C. Fenton, *Saint Matthew* (London 1963).

17 See G. Barth in Bornkamm, op. cit., p. 81; cf. also G. Held in the same volume, p. 257.

18 Bultmann, *History*, etc., p. 147; also his art. *eleos* in *TWNT* II (Stuttgart 1950); cf. also A. H. McNeile, *The Gospel according to Matthew* (London 1938), who identifies *pistis* here with *'emeth* or *'emūnāh*; so also Bornkamm, op. cit., p. 26.

19 See Boismard, op. cit., p. 79, Compare also a phrase which occurs in Eph. 2.4; 1 Pet. 1.3; and Titus 3.5. Common to all these passages is the description of God as rich in mercy or as showing great mercy. I have argued elsewhere that these three passages are all quoting a common tradition of baptismal prayer (see my *Studies in the Pastoral Epistles* (London

1968), pp. 78–96). It seems very likely that Bultmann is right when he claims that the phrase lying behind these three passages is *rab ḥesed* (see Bultmann, art. *eleos*).

20 C. Spicq, *Les Épitres Pastorales* (4 e., Paris 1969); J. Jeremias, *Die Briefe an Timotheus und Titus* (Göttingen 1963); cf. also M. Dibelius and H. Conzelmann, *Die Pastoralbriefe* in loc.

21 J. N. D. Kelly, *The Pastoral Epistles* (London 1963).

22 See an art. by Dr Morna Hooker in *Theology* (November 1972), pp. 570f, 'On Using the Wrong Tool', in which she claims that there are no agreed criteria by which we can distinguish what goes back to Jesus from what was invented by the early Church.

23 Generally speaking, my authorities are J. Jeremias, W. D. Davies, and B. Gerhardsson. What follows has already appeared in an expanded form in my inaugural lecture *Paul's Understanding of Jesus* (Hull 1963), pp. 13–16. See also W. G. Kümmel, *The Theology of the NT* (ET, London 1974, of German e. of 1972), chap. 1, where a similar interpretation is put forward.

24 I am aware that there is some doubt as to whether the word 'unprofitable' formed part of the original text. But the point stands in any case.

25 The lost sheep parable must also be from Q material, since it is also found in Matthew.

26 I regard verse 35 as an editorial addition. In other parts of the New Testament we meet a much more profound doctrine of retribution.

27 For an illuminating discussion of these issues see John Baillie, *The Idea of Revelation in Recent Thought* (Oxford 1956); J. S. Lawton, *Miracles and Revelation* (London 1959).

CHAPTER 2

1 See Karl Barth, *Church Dogmatics: Doctrine of Reconciliation* 1 (ET, Edinburgh 1936–62), p. 134.

2 See C. F. D. Moule, art. 'Further Reflexions on Philippians 2.5–11' in *Apostolic History and the Gospel*, ed. W. W. Gasque and R. P. Martin (Exeter 1970), pp. 264–76.

3 See S. Sykes and J. Clayton, ed., *Christ, Faith, and History* (Cambridge 1972), p. 97.

4 See J. Jeremias, art. *pais theou* in *TWNT* v (Stuttgart 1954), p. 708

5 I am aware that Professor J. Carmignac has recently published a careful lexicographical study to prove that in the phrase *oukh harpagmon hēgēsato* ('did not think it robbery') the negative must be taken with the noun and not the verb, so as to give the sense 'he thought equality with God to be not-robbery', i.e. his undoubted right. See art. 'L'Importance de la place d'une negation (Philippiens ii.6)' in *NTS* (January 1972), pp. 131–66. But even if we concede the force of Professor Carmignac's arguments, I

do not think this necessarily conflicts with Professor Moule's interpretation. We could understand the sentence to mean: 'He regarded divine status as not-snatching, but on the contrary giving.'

6 This interpretation would undercut P. Schoonenberg's understanding of this passage. He takes *harpagmos* as 'something yet to be acquired' and claims that the self-emptying consisted in choosing a servant's life on the human plane rather than choosing the human condition. See art. 'The Kenosis or Self-Emptying of Christ' in *Concilium* (January 1966), pp. 27–36.

7 G. Stählin, art. *asthenēs* in *TWNT* I.

8 H. L. Goudge, *The First Epistle to the Corinthians* (London 1903). See also Conzelmann's comment in H. Conzelmann, *Der erste Brief an die Korinther* (Göttingen 1969) in loc.

9 E.-B. Allo, *Seconde Épitre aux Corinthiens* (Paris 1956).

10 Allo's carefully argued suggestion that it refers to frequently recurring attacks of malaria is certainly attractive.

11 R. P. C. Hanson, *II Corinthians* (London 1954); J. Héring, *La Seconde Épitre aux Corinthiens* (Neuchâtel and Paris 1958).

12 R. H. Strachan, *The Second Epistle of Paul to the Corinthians* (London 1935).

13 See E. Käsemann, *The Testament of Jesus* (ET, London 1968, of German e. of 1966), pp. 47–9.

14 Käsemann, op. cit., p. 53.

15 On this see W. A. Meeks, *The Prophet-King: Moses Traditions in the Johannine Christology* (Leiden 1967), p. 164, where it is suggested that the demand for signs was a demand that Jesus should be a prophet like Moses.

16 R. Schnackenburg, *The Gospel according to John* (ET, London 1967, of German e. of 1965), p. 519. See also K. H. Rengstorf, art. *sēmeion* in *TWNT* VII (Stuttgart 1964).

17 Käsemann, op. cit., p. 22.

18 B. F. Westcott, *The Gospel according to St John* (London 1908); J. H. Bernard, *The Gospel according to St John* (Edinburgh 1928).

19 See Westcott, Bernard, R. H. Bultmann, *Das Evangelium des Johannes* (10 e., Göttingen 1941), p. 239, my tr.; C. H. Dodd, *The Interpretation of the Fourth Gospel* (Cambridge 1960), p. 95; J. Marsh, *Saint John* (London 1968); J. N. Sanders, *The Gospel according to St John* (London 1968); R. Schnackenburg, *Das Johannes-Evangelium*, vol. 2 (Freiburg; Basel; Vienna 1971).

20 C. K. Barrett, *The Gospel according to St John* (London 1955) on 17.21. William Temple also commits himself to this view: 'The unity which the Lord prays that his disciples my enjoy is tahat which is eternally char-

acteristic of the Tri-une God.' See W. M. Temple, *Readings in St John's Gospel* (complete e., London 1947), p. 320.

21   See H. Oppenheimer, *Incarnation and Immanence* (London 1973), p. 211.

22   Compare also Hoskyns' comment; see E. Hoskyns, *The Fourth Gospel* (2 e., London 1947).

23   See K. Rahner, *The Trinity* (ET, London 1970, of German e. of 1967), p. 62.

24   M.-J. Lagrange, *Évangile selon Saint Jean* (3 e., Paris 1927). But the argument from the use of tenses cannot be pressed too far, since the precosmic glory of verse 24 is one which God *has given*, and God *has loved* the Son from all eternity.

25   Käsemann, op. cit., p. 18.

26   W. H. Cadman, *The Open Heaven* (ed. G. B. Caird, Oxford 1969), pp. 110, 163. Compare also C. Welch, *The Trinity in Contemporary Theology* (London 1953), p. 265: 'The assumption that the personal relations between Christ and the Father may be read off as personal relationships within the Godhead seems to be inextricably involved with a defective Christology.' It is interesting to observe that the Lateran Council of 1215 definitely stated that John 17.22 has a different meaning when applied to Christians from what it has when applied to the union between the Father and the Son; the former is a union of grace and love, the latter an identity of nature. The Lateran Fathers have neatly pin-pointed the problem! (See E. J. Fortman, *The Triune God* (Philadelphia 1972), p. 200.) I do not think that even Schoonenberg's attempt to read off consubstantiality from the self-giving quality of Christ's life is justified: 'Thus Christ's self-emptying, down to and including his death on the cross, pre-eminently reveals his equality and unity with the being of the Father, who is love' —see art. cit., p. 36. It is remarkable that Augustine faced the problem posed by a passage such as John 17.23 and answers with great perspicacity: 'The Father and the Son are one not only by equality of substance but also by will' (*De Trinitate*, Bk. IX, ix, 18, ed. M. Mellet and Th. Camelot, vol. 15 (Bruges 1955)).

27   Some would translate *kai eisakoustheis apo tēs eulabeias* as 'and being heard [and delivered from] the fear [of death]'. I reject this rendering for the following reasons: (*a*) the verb *eisakouein* cannot bear this double meaning; (*b*) the author means that Christ was saved from ultimate (though not physical) death by the resurrection; (*c*) the Synoptic narratives represent Jesus in Gethsemane as praying (subject to the Father's will) for deliverance from death, not from the fear of death.

28   K. Rahner, op. cit., pp. 27–33; see also his *Theological Investigations* 4 (ET, London 1960, of German e. of 1960), p. 94.

29   Bultmann, op. cit., p. 41, my tr.

30   Quoted in R. V. Sellers, *The Council of Chalcedon* (London 1953), p. 191.

31 Quoted from H. Bettenson, *Documents of the Christian Church* (Oxford 1943), p. 72.

32 The Transfiguration might be considered to approximate to this. Most remarkably, John does not mention it. For a most valuable discussion of the relation between the Christian concept of the incarnation and the *avatār* cult of Hindu religious tradition see G. Parrinder, *Avatar and Incarnation* (London 1970). It is surprising that he makes no reference to the Transfiguration.

33 See my *Jesus Christ in the Old Testament* (London 1965), pp. 141–4.

34 Justin is in fact the earliest witness to this rabbinic interpretation of Ps. 24. There is plenty of later testimony to it; see W. G. Braude, *Midrash on the Psalms* I (New Haven 1959) in loc.

35 The older commentators tend to follow the first solution, e.g., Robertson-Plummer and Goudge; the second solution is favoured by Chrysostom and Theodoret.

36 E.g., Weiss, Evans, Allo, Héring, Barrett, Conzelmann.

37 E. Evans, *The First Epistle of Paul the Apostle to the Corinthians* (Oxford 1930).

38 J. Weiss, *Der Erste Korintherbrief* (16 e., Göttingen 1910).

39 J. B. Lightfoot, *The Apostolic Fathers*, ed. J. R. Harmer (London 1891), pp. 141–2.

CHAPTER 3

1 See *Church Dogmatics: the Doctrine of Reconciliation* I, p. 236.

2 A. Weiser, *Das Buch Jeremia* (Göttingen 1966).

3 W. Rudolph, *Jeremia* (Tübingen 1968).

4 See A. Aeschimann, *Le Prophète Jérémie* (Neuchâtel and Paris 1959).

5 J. Bright, *Jeremiah* (New York 1965), introd.

6 Weiser, op. cit., introd., p. xxviii.

7 H. L. Strack and P. Billerbeck, *Komm. z. N.T. aus Talmud und Midrasch* (3 e., Munich 1961) in loc. Matt. 16.14.

8 M.-J. Lagrange, *Évangile selon Matthieu* (Paris 1948) in loc. Matt. 16.14.

9 He was said to have been born circumcised and to have been descended from a marriage between Joshua and Rahab. For these references see *Tractate Ta'anith* 22b (113), ed. J. Rabbinowitz (London 1938); *Tractate Megillah* 14b (85), ed. M. Simon (London 1938); *Tractate 'Arakin* 12b (69), ed. L. Jung (London 1949); *Tractate Kallah Rabbathi* 53b (471), ed. A. Cohen in *Minor Tractates of the Talmud* (London 1965).

10 E.g., A. C. Welch, *Jeremiah, his Time and Work* (Oxford 1951), p. 42.

11 For Psalm references see Rom. 3.10f; 8.36; 15.3, 9, 11; 2 Cor. 4.13; Eph. 4.8.

12   D. M. Baillie, *God Was in Christ* (London 1947), p. 131; W. N. Pittenger, *The Word Incarnate* (London 1959), p. 195.

13   Karl Barth, *Doctrine of the Word of God* 1, 2, p. 62.

14   If this topic were treated fully, the Book of Job would have to come into consideration, a Book which has links both with Jeremiah and the servant of Second Isaiah. The author rejected the Deuteronomic doctrine of theodicy, but did not (not clearly at any rate) have any inkling of the new dimension. The result seems to be a riddle rather than a solution.

15   See R. V. Sellers, *Two Ancient Christologies* (London 1940), p. 59.

16   Compare A. E. Garvie, *The Christian Doctrine of the Godhead* (London 1925), p. 148. See also W. L. Walker, *The Gospel of Reconciliation* (Edinburgh 1909), p. 169.

CHAPTER 4

1   E.g. Jude 5, where four Greek uncials, several Old Latin MSS, the Vulgate and the Ethiopic, Jerome and Cyril read *Iēsous* instead of *Kurios* or *ho theos*. The RSV in an effort to avoid committing itself reads 'he who saved . . .', thereby translating a reading which, as far as I know, is not represented by any extant MS.

2   J. M. Creed, *The Divinity of Jesus Christ* (1964 e. of original e. of 1938), pp. 122–3.

3   D. M. Baillie, op. cit., p. 68.

4   See Karl Rahner, *Theological Investigations* 1 (ET, London 1961, of German e. of 1954), p. 136.

5   A good example of the ambiguity which occurs when *theos* is applied indiscriminately to Christ occurs in Titus 1.3, where 'by command of God our Saviour' might refer either to the Father or the Son.

6   Op. cit., p. 167.

7   I have examined this doctrine as far as it appears in the New Testament in *Jesus Christ in the Old Testament*.

8   See *The Human Face of God* (London 1973), pp. 147–8.

9   See *Jesus Christ in the Old Testament*, pp. 48–82. Dr Robinson does not appear to have noticed this book.

10   J. A. T. Robinson's treatment of Paul, Hebrews, and John will be found on pp. 155–79 of his book.

11   I have deliberately followed the NEB translation here. The RSV 'rejoiced that he was to see my day' seems to be less accurate.

12   See J. Macquarrie, art. 'The Pre-existence of Jesus Christ' in *Expository Times* (April 1960), pp. 199–202.

13   P. Schoonenberg, *The Christ* (ET, London 1972, of Dutch e. of 1969),

pp. 57, 80. See also art. 'God's Presence in Jesus: an exchange of viewpoints' in *Theology Digest*, vol. XIX, no. 1 (Spring 1971), pp. 24–38.

14 Probably 'in the mode of Son' is the best rendering of *en huiō/i* in Heb. 1.2: 'in a Son' suggests that there might be more than one, and there is no textual support for 'in the Son' or 'in his Son.

15 Personally I would put it after rather than before A.D. 70.

16 See *Studies in Paul's Technique and Theology* (London 1974), pp. 39–51.

17 The Latin word for *epieikeia* is *clementia*, and the 'Clementia Caesaris' was elevated into a cult in the state religion of the Roman Empire. But this too was the clemency of the victor for the vanquished. See S. Weinstock, *Divus Julius* (Oxford 1971), pp. 233–43. See on this passage in 2 Corinthians C. K. Barrett, *The Second Letter to the Corinthians* (London 1973), where the view taken here is defended.

18 E.g. A. B. Bruce, W. L. Walker, H. J. Mackintosh, and A. E. Garvie.

19 This is John Knox's solution; see his book *The Humanity and Divinity of Christ* (Cambridge 1967).

20 This view is associated with the names (among others) of W. L. Knox, W. D. Davies, and A. Feuillet.

21 I have elaborated this argument in *Studies in Paul's Technique and Theology*, pp. 221–57.

22 For a clear example of this, see Karl Barth's account of the incarnation discussed in the next chapter.

23 W. Pannenberg *Jesus: God and Man* (ET, London 1968, of German e. of 1964), p. 131.

24 Ibid., pp. 69–70, 106.

25 J. McIntyre, *The Shape of Christology* (London 1966), pp. 164, 168.

26 Pannenberg, op. cit., p. 160.

27 Pittenger, *The Word Incarnate*, p. 130.

28 It is true that on p. 177 Pittenger writes of God: 'He *is* of course, but his innermost nature is declared to be loving will or (perhaps better phrased) purposive love.' But this is not worked out in terms of ontology.

29 See *Doctrine of the Word of God* 1, 2, p. 397.

30 See especially p. 217.

31 See *The Christ*, p. 99.

32 See art. 'God's Presence in Jesus', p. 35.

33 See *Incarnation and Immanence*, pp. 35, 61.

34 Most modern editors seem to prefer the reading *monogenēs theos* in 1.18 to *monogenēs huios*. In fact there is much to be said for reading *ho monogenēs* alone, as witnessed by some MSS. of the Vulgate and a considerable number of Fathers. I assume that the prologue has ended before 1.34.

35 See E. J. Fortman, *The Triune God*, p. 211.

36 L. Hodgson, *The Doctrine of the Trinity* (London 1943).

37 See D. M. Baillie, op. cit., p. 136. Dr Oppenheimer also inclines to follow Hodgson; see op. cit. pp. 204–9. She does jib at allowing three centres of consciousness. She does not take any notice of Barth's approach nor indeed of Pannenberg's, which at certain points comes very close to her own. Is there, one wonders, an integral connection between her holding a doctrine of the Trinity which verges towards Tritheism and her extreme difficulty in formulating the mode of the hypostatic union? See the discussion of this in the next chapter, and also C. Welch's remark quoted in note 26 of Chapter 2. See also D. M. Baillie, op. cit., p. 136.

38 For the quotation see *The Trinity*, p. 109, and for his critique of 'Person' see pp. 105f. He discusses Barth's phrase on p. 44.

39 See *Theological Investigations* 1, p. 146.

40 *Jesus: God and Man*, pp. 180–3.

41 See an interesting discussion of this problem in R. P. C. Hanson, *The Attractiveness of God* (London 1973), pp. 116–37. I entirely agree with him that to characterize the Holy Spirit as the bond of love between the Father and the Son is unsatisfactory. See also C. Welch, op. cit., pp. 286–90. He rightly repudiates the notion that the Son is peculiarly the object of the Father's love.

42 *Theological Investigations* 4 (ET, London 1966, of German e. of 1960), p. 115.

43 *The Trinity*, pp. 101–2.

44 See *De Trinitate*, Bk. v, ix, 10 *Dictum est ne taceretur*. Augustine is discussing the nature of the Persons of the Trinity. The full quotation runs thus: 'But when we are asked, "Three what?", we encounter at once a huge deficiency in human language. However, we say "Three Persons", not for the sake of saying it, but because the only alternative is silence', my tr.

45 See *The Problem of Christ in the Twentieth Century*, pp. 65–6. 70–1.

46 See *Incarnation and Immanence*, pp. 161, 164.

47 See *Theological Investigations* 3 (ET, London 1967, of German e. of 1956), p. 44.

48 See *The Christ*, pp. 169–70.

49 E. Schweizer, art *sōma* in *TWNT* vii (Stuttgart 1964).

50 See *Incarnation and Immanence*, p. 218.

51 I only consider examples of worship offered before Jesus' resurrection. Matthew uses *proskunein* seven times in this context; Mark only once, Mark 5.6, where worship is offered by a madman; but this is probably intended to be Satan's tribute and does not tell us how humans behaved. There is one clear instance in the Fourth Gospel, John 9.38, when the man cured of blindness worships Jesus, an act of worship which Jesus accepts. There are no instances in Luke.

CHAPTER 5

1   Quoted from H. R. Bettenson, *Documents of the Christian Church*, p. 73.

2   The meaning of *hupostasis* is well brought out by McIntyre, op. cit., pp. 95f.

3   This is at least the conclusion I draw from A. R. Vine's learned study of *The Bazaar of Heracleides* called *An Approach to Christology* (London 1948).

4   See Sellers, *The Council of Chalcedon*, pp. xv, 8, 171.

5   Sellers insists that *invicem* in the *Tome* means 'in relation to each other' not 'alternately', but my criticism still holds (op. cit., p. 237).

6   Bettenson, op. cit., p. 72.

7   This is very much the way in which the Antiochenes understood the operation of the two natures: 'the Logos allowed the manhood to experience what belongs to it', quoted in Sellers, op. cit., p. 171.

8   For 'dividing the sayings' see Sellers, op. cit., p. 23; for the reference to Cyril see p. 150; and for Sellers' own claim p. 202.

9   G. Gore, ed., *Lux Mundi* (London 1890), p. 237.

10 J. R. Illingworth, *Personality Human and Divine* (London 1894), p. 198.

11 See E. G. Selwyn, ed., *Essays Catholic and Critical*, pp. 190–1, 195, 196, 198.

12 His treatment of the subject is to be found in the first two hundred pages of his *Doctrine of the Word of God* 1, 2, but his preparatory material in the previous volume is also illuminating. See 1, 1, pp. 321–2 (ET, Edinburgh 1956).

13 1, 1, p. 460.

14 See John Knox, *The Humanity and Divinity of Jesus Christ*, pp. 5f; P. Schoonenberg, *The Christ*, p. 114.

15 'He assumes the nature but not the person': the reference is 2, p. 250.

16 H. M. Relton, *A Study in Christology* (London 1934).

17 I would pass the same judgement on A. R. Vine's book referred to in n.3 above. He writes a few sentences protesting that he is not committed to accepting literally everything John wrote (p. 398), but in effect his picture of the incarnate Word is largely taken from the Fourth Gospel.

18 See *The Council of Chalcedon*, pp. 345, 347

19 See *Incarnation and Immanence*, pp. 212, 214, 215, 216.

20 See D. M. Baillie, *God Was in Christ*, p. 87.

21 See W. N. Pittenger, *The Word Incarnate*, p. 32.

22 See also W. N. Pittenger, *Christology Reconsidered* (London 1970), pp. 66, 68, 99, 135. This approach is rejected by Pannenberg, *Jesus: God and Man*, pp. 22 and 48; and is criticized by D. M. Mackinnon (see S. Sykes and J. Clayton, ed., *Christ, Faith, and History*, p. 292); R. S. Barbour in his

little book *Traditio-Historical Criticism of the Gospels* (London 1972) has submitted this view to a most damaging criticism (see pp. 42–5).

23 See Karl Rahner, *Theological Investigations* I, pp, 149f.

24 I have not discussed P. Schoonenberg's more radical treatment of the incarnation, because I cannot see that his position differs very much from that advocated in this book; nor do I understand how he can reconcile it with acceptance of the Chalcedonian Formula. See *The Christ*, pp. 72–140.

25 See Chapter 4, section 2.

26 For an interesting discussion of the possibility of alternative theologies coexisting within an all-embracing norm of faith, see James Barr, *The Bible in the Modern World* (London 1973), esp. pp. 114, 133, 136.

BIBLIOGRAPHY

BOOKS REFERRED TO IN TEXT

Aeschimann, A., *Le Prophète Jérémie.* Neuchâtel & Paris 1959.
Allo, E.-B., *Seconde Épitre aux Corinthiens.* Paris 1936.
Baillie, D. M., *God Was in Christ.* London 1947.
Baillie, J., *The Idea of Revelation in Recent Thought.* Oxford 1956.
Barbour, R. S., *Traditio-Historical Criticism of the Gospels.* London 1972.
Barr, J., *The Bible in the Modern World.* London 1973.
Barrett, C. K., *The Gospel according to Saint John.* London 1955.
— *The Second Letter to the Corinthians.* London 1973.
Barth, K., *Church Dogmatics: Doctrine of Reconciliation.* ET, London 1936–62.
Baumgartner, W., *see* Koehler, L.
Bernard, J. H., *The Gospel according to St John.* Edinburgh 1928.
Bettenson, H., *Documents of the Christian Church.* Oxford 1943.
Bewer, J. A., *The Book of Jonah.* Edinburgh 1912.
Billerbeck, P., *see* Strack, H. L.
Boismard, M.-E., *Le Prologue de Saint Jean.* Paris 1953.
Bornkamm, G., ed., *Tradition and Interpretation in Matthew.* ET, London 1963.
Braude, W. G., *Midrash on the Psalms,* vol. i. New Haven 1959.
Bright, J., *Jeremiah.* New York 1965.
Bultmann, R., *Das Evangelium des Johannes.* 10 e., Göttingen 1941.
— *History of the Synoptic Tradition.* ET, London 1968.
Cadman, W. H., *The Open Heaven.* Oxford 1969.
Camelot, T., *see* Mellet, M.
Clayton, J., *see* Sykes, S.
Cohen, A., *Tractate Kallah Rabbathi* in *Minor Tractates of the Talmud.* London 1965.
Conzelmann, H., *see* Dibelius, M.
— *Die Erste Brief an die Korinther.* Göttingen 1969.
Creed, J. M., *The Divinity of Jesus Christ.* Cambridge 1938.
Dibelius, M., and Conzelmann, H., *Die Pastoralbriefe.* Tübingen 1955.

Dodd, C. H., *The Interpretation of the Fourth Gospel.* Cambridge 1960.
Epstein, I., ed., *The Babylonian Talmud.* London 1935+.
Etheridge, J. W., *The Targum of Onkelos and Jonathan ben Uzziel.* New e., New York 1968.
Evans, E., *The First Epistle of Paul to the Corinthians.* Oxford 1930.
Fenton, J. C., *Saint Matthew.* London 1963.
Fortnam, E. J., *The Triune God.* Philadelphia 1972.
Garvie, A. E., *The Christian Doctrine of the Godhead.* London 1925.
Glueck, N., *Hesed in the Bible.* New e., Cincinnati 1967.
Gore, C., ed., *Lux Mundi.* London 1890.
Goudge, H. L., *The First Epistle to the Corinthians.* London 1903.
Hanson, A. T., *Paul's Understanding of Jesus.* Hull 1963.
— *Jesus Christ in the Old Testament.* London 1965.
— *Studies in the Pastoral Epistles.* London 1968.
— *Studies in Paul's Technique and Theology.* London 1974.
Hanson, R. P. C., *II Corinthians.* London 1954.
— *The Attractiveness of God.* London 1973.
Héring, J., *La Seconde Épitre aux Corinthiens.* Neuchâtel & Paris.
Hodgson, L., *The Doctrine of the Trinity.* London 1943.
Hoskyns, E., *The Fourth Gospel.* 2 e., London 1947.
Illingworth, J. R., *Personality, Human and Divine.* London 1894.
Jeremias, J., *Die Briefe an Timotheus und Titus.* Göttingen 1963.
Jung, L., *Tractate 'Arakin* in *The Babylonian Talmud.* London 1949.
Käsemann, E., *The Testament of Jesus.* ET, London 1968.
Kelly, J. N. D., *The Pastoral Epistles.* London 1963.
Knox, J., *The Humanity and Divinity of Christ.* Cambridge 1967.
Koehler, L., and Baumgarten, W., *Lexicon in Veteris Testamenti Libros.* Leiden 1953.
Kümmel, W. G., *The Theology of the New Testament.* ET, London 1974.
Lagrange, M.-J., *Évangile selon Saint Jean.* 3 e., Paris 1927.
— *Évangile selon Matthieu.* Paris 1948.
Lawton, J. S., *Miracles and Revelation.* London 1959.
Lightfoot, J. B., *The Apostolic Fathers.* London 1891.
Lohmeyer, E., *Das Evangelium Matthäus.* Göttingen 1962.
Marsh, J., *Saint John.* London 1968.
Matthews, W. R., *The Problem of Christ in the Twentieth Century.* London 1950.
McIntyre, J., *The Shape of Christology.* London 1966.
McNeile, A. H., *The Gospel according to Matthew.* London 1938.
Meeks, W. A., *The Prophet-King: Moses Traditions in the Johannine Christology.* Leiden 1967.

Mellet, M., and Camelot, T., ed., *Augustine's De Trinitate*. Bruges 1955.
Montefiore, C. G., *The Synoptic Gospels*. London 1909.
Oppenheimer, H., *Incarnation and Immanence*. London 1973.
Pannenberg, W., *Jesus: God and Man*. ET, London 1968.
Parrinder, G., *Avatar and Incarnation*. London 1970.
Pittenger, W. N., *The Word Incarnate*. London 1959.
— *Christology Reconsidered*. London 1970.
Plummer, A., *see* Robertson, A.
Rabbinowitz, J., *Tractate Ta'anith* in *The Babylonian Talmud*. London 1938.
Rahner, K., *The Trinity*. ET, London 1970.
— *Theological Investigations* 1 ET, London 1961.
— *Theological Investigations* 3 ET, London 1967.
— *Theological Investigations* 4 ET, London 1960.
Relton, H. M., *A Study in Christology*. London 1934.
Rigaux, B., *Témoinage de L'Évangile de Matthieu*. Brussels 1967.
Robertson, A., and Plummer, A., *A Critical and Exegetical Commentary on the First Epistle of Paul to the Corinthians*. Edinburgh 1911.
Robinson, J. A. T., *The Human Face of God*. London 1973.
Rudolph, W., *Jeremia*. Tübingen 1968.
— *Das Buch Jonas*. Gütersloh 1971.
Sanders, J. N., *The Gospel according to St John*. London 1968.
Schnackenburg, R., *The Gospel according to John*, vol. 1. ET, London 1967.
— *Das Johannes-Evangelium*, vol. 2. Freiburg, Basel, Vienna 1971.
Schoonenberg, P., *The Christ*. ET, London 1972.
Sellers, R. V., *Two Ancient Christologies*. London 1940.
— *The Council of Chalcedon*. London 1953.
Selwyn, E. G., *Essays Catholic and Critical*. 3 e., London 1931.
Simon, M., *Tractate Megillah* in *The Babylonian Talmud*. London 1958.
— *Tractate Rosh Hashanah* in *The Babylonian Talmud*. London 1938.
Slotki, W., *Tractate 'Erubin* in *The Babylonian Talmud*. London 1938.
Spicq, C., *Les Épitres Pastorales*. Paris 1969.
Strachan, R. H., *The Second Epistle of Paul to the Corinthians*. London 1935.
Strack, H. L., and Billerbeck, P., *Komm z. N.T. aus Talmud und Midrasch*. 3 e., Munich 1961.
Sykes, S., and Clayton, J., *Christ, Faith, and History*. Cambridge 1972.
Temple, W. M., *Readings in St. John's Gospel*. London 1947.
Vine, A. R., *An Approach to Christology*. London 1948.
Walker, W. L., *The Gospel of Reconciliation*. Edinburgh 1909.

Weinstock, S., *Divus Julius*. Oxford 1971.
Weiser, A., *Das Buch der zwölf kleinen Propheten*. Göttingen 1963.
— *Das Buch Jeremia*. Göttingen 1963.
Weiss, J., *Der Erste Korintherbrief*. 16 e., Göttingen 1910.
Welch, A. C., *Jeremiah, his Time and Work*. Oxford 1951.
Welch, C., *The Trinity in Contemporary Theology*. London 1953.
Westcott, B. F., *The Gospel according to St John*. London 1908.

ARTICLES REFERRED TO IN THE TEXT

Bultmann, R., art. *alētheia* in *TWNT*, vol. I. Stuttgart 1949.
— art. *eleos* in *TWNT*, vol. II. Stuttgart 1950.
Carmignac, J., 'L'Importance de la place d'une negation (Philippiens ii.6)' in *NTS* (Jan. 1972), pp. 131f.
Hooker, M., 'On Using the Wrong Tool' in *Theology* (Nov. 1972), pp. 570f.
Jeremias, J., art. *pais theou* in *TWNT*, vol. V. Stuttgart 1954.
Johnson, A., 'Hesed and Hasid' in *Interpretationes ad Vetus Testamentum pertinentes Sigmundo Mowinckel septuagenario missae* (Oslo 1955), pp. 101f.
Kuyper, L. J., 'Grace and Truth: an Old Testament Description of God and Its Use in the Johannine Gospel' in *The Reformed Review* (Sept. 1962).
Leclerque, H., 'A Note on the Transliteration of New Testament Greek' in *NTS* (Jan. 1973), pp. 187f.
Mackinnon, D. M., art. in *Christ, Faith, and History*. *See* Sykes, S.
Macquarrie, J., 'The Pre-Existence of Jesus Christ' in *Expository Times* (Apr. 1960), pp. 199f.
Moule, C. F. D., 'Further Reflections on Philippians 2.5–11' in *Apostolic History and the Gospel*, ed. W. W. Gasque and R. P. Martin. London 1970.
— art. in *Christ, Faith, and History*. *See* Sykes, S.
Rengstorf, K. H., art. *sēmeion* in *TWNT*, vol. VII. Stuttgart 1964.
Schoonenberg, P., 'The Kenosis or Self-Emptying of Christ' in *Concilium* (Jan. 1966), pp. 27f.
— 'God's Presence in Christ' in *Theology Digest* (Spring 1971), pp. 24f.
Schweizer, E., art. *sōma* in *TWNT*, vol. VII. Stuttgart 1964.
Stählin, G., art. *asthenēs* in *TWNT*, vol. I. Stuttgart 1949.
Weingreen, J., 'Some Observations on English Versions of the Old Testament' in *Hermathena* (Summer 1972), pp. 12f.

INDEX OF NAMES

INDEX OF SCRIPTURE REFERENCES